POKE LOKE

Stories of Growing Up in the 1940s and 1950s

Johnny Norwood

Published September 2021 by

MULTIPLYING MINISTRIES

Training Others to Train Others

2 Timothy 2:2

DEDICATION

These writings, recollections, and ramblings are dedicated to my family. Y'all better read it, because I put a lot of time and energy into it. You might consider buying some copies for your friends (since they probably won't buy it for themselves).

I love and am so proud of each of you -
1 wife, 3 kids and their 3 mates, 8 grands (and 4 mates), and 1 great-grand-daughter:
    Diana, Noel, Molly, Johnathan, Michaela, Carl, Mikaila, Amelia Grace, Elliott, Eric, April, Mark, Shelby, Kayla, Kris, Jana, Aaron, Cheyenne, Seth, and Joel, plus all who will join the family later, by birth or marriage.

ENDORSEMENTS

These endorsers offered no objection to being quoted:

Adam –	*My wife made me read it.*
Noah –	*I read it on my cruise.*
Abraham –	*I believed it.*
Sarah –	*It made me laugh.*
Joseph –	*I dreamed about it.*
Moses –	*I'd cross the Red Sea to read it again.*
Samson –	*This is not long-hair stuff.*
Jonah –	*At first, I refused, but later I read it.*
Solomon –	*It contains much wisdom.*
Isaiah –	*I prophesy it will become a best-seller.*
Daniel –	*I read it while relaxing in my den.*
Matthew –	*It's not taxing.*
Zaccheus –	*I read the short version.*
Bartimaeus –	*I needed the Braille version, until I met Jesus.*
Luke –	*It was medicine for my soul.*
Barnabas –	*It is very encouraging.*
Paul –	*I read it in jail.*

ACKNOWLEDGMENTS

Editing by Mark Whiteout
Cover Design by Drew Poorly
Marketing by Willy Regreddit
Proof Reading by Kantz Pellet
Grammar Checking by Skip Toverett
Lawyers (in case of libel suits) - Sly Shark, Wilby D. Bard, Ima D. Seaver, and Freda Crook.

FORWARD

Having searched diligently for someone to write a somewhat positive forward, I finally come up with a reluctant victim. My lifelong acquaintance, John O. Nonwordy, has concocted his impressions of my book. I am deeply indebted to him (referring to my pocketbook). Mr. Nonwordy writes as follows:

I eventually finished reading what's-his-name's manuscript, editing out multiple errors, typos, and inaccuracies. There were a bunch of them. I also scratched out some "inappropriatenesses," outright lies, as well as the really boring stuff - although I might have missed some. I can highly recommend that you buy this book, because I will get a commission. It's up to you whether you read it or not.

DISCLAIMERS

Before you delve into the adventures, a few disclaimers are in order.
1. Most of the characters you will meet have undergone a name change and a slight personality modification. This is done to protect me from liability or revenge or worse.
2. All of the stories are true, to the best of my memory, which is not as sharp now as in days past.
3. Some of you who grew up with me are not mentioned. Hey, I couldn't include all of you. Sorry.
4. I wasn't the one that set that fire.

SMORGASBORD OF DELECTABLES
(LIST OF STUFF)

INTRODUCTION TO <u>POKE LORE</u> 6
GROWING UP IN POKE COUNTY 7
HOW I GOT HERE 12
THE HOUSTON YEARS 21
WHAT WERE THINGS LIKE IN THE 1940s? ... 24
THE HIGHWAY 59 YEARS 29
THE HOUSE BY THE TRACKS 35
    Moving to the House By the Tracks 35
    The Great Snake Hunt 37
    The Long, Long Tunnel 39
    The Disastrous Duet 42
    My Dog Butch 44
    Last Chosen 47
    Paper Boxes 48
    Small-Town Entertainment 52
    The Whuppin' 57
    Watching Radio 60
    The Really Cool Hammock 65
    The Snake that Almost Killed Me 68
WHAT WERE THINGS LIKE IN THE 1950s? 70
THE HOUSE ON CALHOUN 77
    Moving to Calhoun Street 77
    My Back Yard 79
    The Turkey Give-Away 89
    Facing A Timber Rattler 92
    The Batting Range 94
    Snipes and Yipes 97
    Boy Scouting – The Camping Years 101
    Tornado Trauma 106
    The Big Treehouse 108
    The Teacher Is Here 119
    More Boy Scouting 122
    You Have A Dentist Appointment 127
    Mauled By a Bobcat 131

Mayhaws, Chinkypins, and More 134
Darkness to Dawning 137
Baseball – My First Love 139
My High School Football Career 147
Central Baptist Church 154
My High School Teachers 160
TIDBITS THROUGH THE YEARS 167
   Gertrude and Neelie 167
   Television in the 1950s 171
   Latch-Key Kid 175
FINDING A CAREER 177
WHERE DO YOU STOP? 181
LEAVING POKE COUNTY 184

INTRODUCTION TO POKE LORE

Dad, Mom, and I zipped down two-lane Highway 59, from Livingston toward Houston, in our ten-year-old 1939 Ford two-door sedan, or Tudor Sedan as Ford nicknamed it. The vehicle bounced and rattled over the pot holes, and so did we. Light traffic early that Saturday morning tempted Dad to exceed the speed limit. Suddenly, we heard the siren and saw the flashing lights. I was terrified.

"Sir, let me see your license," the patrolman demanded. Being only seven years old, my terror ratcheted up a notch.

"Howdy, aw-fi-sur," my dad replied, and showed his license. "Wur frum Poke County."

Two notes here. First, we East Texans have a unique drawl. I remained unaware of that fact until I left Livingston for college, where even fellow Southerners laughed at my dialect and accent. Second, I was in high school before I understood that we lived in Polk, not "Poke," County. Poke is how I learned to pronounce it.

"From 'Poke' County, huh?" The officer softened his voice in a condescending way. "Well, you need to slow down a little and enjoy the big city. I'll let you go with a warning - this time."

I had just gained a valuable lesson - how to play dumb to avoid getting a traffic ticket. Dad used an exaggerated drawl and a slow-witted, open-mouthed expression to perfection. Later, I heard that many Poke County drivers used that same ploy.

The saying went, "If you get stopped near Houston, just tell them you're from Poke County. They'll probably let you go." We Poke Countians weren't as dumb as those city folks thought.

I grew up in the 1940's and 1950's in Livingston, the county-seat town. Those magical years are plum full of memorable stories begging to be told.

Thus, the title of this book - Poke Lore.

GROWING UP IN POKE COUNTY

This is my story of growing up in "Poke" County, Texas, in the 1940's and 50's. I'm in my late 70's as I write, so please make allowance for a sketchy memory, and try not to check too closely on the accuracy of each assertion of fact.

In case you skipped the Introduction on the previous page, go back right now and read it, so I don't have to re-explain some stuff.

Polk County was established in 1846 and named for the sitting president, James K. Polk. It's located in the "piney woods" of deep East Texas, and contains a major portion of a huge, partially unexplored forest/swamp designated Big Thicket National Preserve.

Livingston, my hometown, is the county seat town. We had the county's only traffic light, and boasted a population of some 2,800 during my early years. Everyone knew everyone in Livingston. If a stranger happened into town, observers would say, "Wunder whur he's frum?" Strangers were welcome, we were just curious about them, and wondered how long they would stay.

Moses Livingston Choate founded Livingston in 1836. Historians argue whether he hailed from the Livingston in Alabama or Tennessee. I imagine both cities brag today about their namesake in Polk County. First named Springfield, because of its many springs, the name changed to Livingston in 1846.

Here's the story. In March 1846, a committee was asked to choose a county seat town, so they gave three suggestions - Springfield, Johnson's Bluff, and Swartout. Choate offered 100 acres of land to Polk County if the site of Springfield were chosen, with the stipulation that the name be changed to Livingston. **I'm so glad I didn't have to go through life saying, "I'm from Swartout."**

(Apologies to some of my friends from there.)

City folks called us "country hicks," "back-woods bumpkins," or "local yokels." They even used some terms that were derogatory. We thought they were complimenting us, because we were proud to be residents of such a beautiful, peaceful, piney woods county. Poke County was our home, and we felt sorry for folks who had to suffer life in a big city.

Our neck-of-the-woods comprised of a dozen or more small, picturesque towns connected by paved roads, and innumerable smaller communities nestled along a maze of dirt roads.

You may have heard of some of them:
Point Blank	Seven Oaks
Marston	Ace
Buck	Camp Ruby
Kickapoo	East Tempe
Pluck	Chink
Hortense	

Nope? None of them? Well, I'm sure you've heard of Moscow, Israel, and Asia. They are towns in Polk County too.

Most of these were small sawmill and/or farming communities with interesting stories about their origin.

<u>Midway</u>, an agricultural community, got its name in 1888. Two prominent families fought over where to locate the new schoolhouse, each proposing a site near them and near a spring. A feud threatened, until a third family suggested a compromise – build it midway between them. Thus, the name. However, no spring flowed nearby, so the children had to bring their own drinking water to school.

<u>Soda</u>, a farming and sawmill community, applied for a post office in 1898. Proposed names were submitted, and the Post Office Department chose letters from the suggested names and formed the name, "Soda."

<u>Tin Top</u> began as a small settlement of farmers on Kickapoo Creek. When a school and a church were erected with tin roofs, the community became known as Tin Top.

Barnum, a sawmill town, was named for the P.T. Barnum Circus.

Living in the 1940s and 50s in Poke County was unique and fun. We didn't have any of the modern-day conveniences to worry about - just plain, simple living. Of course, that's what our parents said of their growing up years, before and during the "Roaring Twenties." They called my growing up years "these modern times." I guess every generation says that.

You might be surprised to know that we did have a lot of the twenty-first century stuff - just different definitions for them.

For instance:

I-Pad = A patch you wore over your eye when it got poked and bled.

Cell Phone = What a criminal was allowed to use only once, after being arrested.

Face Book = The imprint an open textbook made on the side of your face when you fell sound asleep in class.

Apple Watch = What you yelled at a friend when someone threw an apple core at him –
as in "Apple Core!" "Baltimore!"

GPS = A folded, paper road map you could get free at a gas station.

Computer = Someone who could do math really fast.

Personal Computer = A friend who would help you with your math homework.

Internet = What you coaxed the fish flopping on the end of your line to do.

Texting = Passing hand-written notes in class.

Safety Belts = What kept the kids secure in the back seat. Not the seatbelts you buckled up, but the kind your dad threatened to unbuckle, take off, and "tan your hide" with if you didn't "straighten up right now."

Dishwasher = You, or preferably a younger sibling.

Clothes Dryer = A cord strung between two trees in the back yard, with a pole in the middle to keep it from sagging.

Remote Control = The knowledge your parents would somehow find out, so you didn't do it.

Home Security System = That which barks and needs to be fed.

Air-Conditioning = In the vehicle, you roll the windows down. In the house, you pull the windows up.

And, come to think of it, Insta-Pot meant something else, too.

Life was idyllic. We ran around barefoot in the summer, and drank water from a hose. We caught lightening bugs and put them in a fruit jar. We played in the creek - and in the dirt, the rain, and the mud.

We played "cops and robbers" and "cowboys and Indians," with sticks for guns and cardboard boxes for forts.

We read comic books, traded baseball cards, played jacks, tiddlywinks, and marbles, and went to Saturday matinee cowboy movies. We rode in the back of our dad's pickup, rode our bikes all over town, and skated on the sidewalks and paved streets. **Those were good times.**

<u>The stories I will tell you are true</u>. Some of the names of individuals might be changed to protect the guilty.

Before we begin the stories, let me warn you about the first one - "How I Got Here" - on the next page. I wrote it mainly for my own family and a few close friends. It's interesting, but not a "page turner," so don't let it discourage you.

Once you start yawning, just skip on over to **My Parents Marriage** on page 20, and continue from there.

However, you'll miss some really good stuff, but it's up to you.

If you want to get a sampling of what 90% of this book will look like, try **The Disastrous Duet** on page 42.

Hope you enjoy reading as much as I enjoyed writing. BTW, there will be sequels to follow – more Lore beyond Poke.

HOW I GOT HERE
1165-1942
My Birth

I came out screaming, and according to my mom, kept it up for several months. That happened at 11:00 p.m. on Monday, May 25, 1942 in Flowers' Hospital, Livingston, Texas. I weighed in at six and one-half pounds. The hospital, annexed to Dr. Flowers' own house, was one of two small hospitals in town. Livingston had a population of 2,300 that year.

Wondering what other events occurred on the day of my birth, I have meticulously researched newspaper archives, which revealed these notable headlines and news reports on 05/25/42:

- In the *St. Louis Times* – "Nest" –
  Mrs. F. W. Duenckel found a newly built robin's nest with a slip of paper hanging over the side, reading: "Please leave an extra quart of milk."

- In the *Atlantic City News* – "Short Cut" –
  Autoist William Minuth collided with an arrow-shaped signpost reading "Hospital," to which he was removed.

- In the *Danville Gazette* – "Out of Control" –
  Lightning struck the home of H. M. Watkins, the weatherman.

- In the *Fairview Enterprise* – "Decision" –
  Members of a local rationing board, who were boys once themselves, refused to let a truant officer buy new tires.

Further research revealed these interesting occurrences on May 25:
- In 240 BC, Halley's Comet was first recorded passing near the sun.
- In 1048 AD, emperor Shenzong of China was born.
- In 1978 AD, *Star Wars* was released.

I'm very disappointed. The list of momentous events and famous births on my birthdate is painfully short. But hey, I just had a thought. Maybe, after I die, someone will include my birth in that short list, and I will become famous.

My Ancestors

Bear with me for a little Norwood family history. Let me introduce:
Sir Stephen DeNorthwode – my 22nd great-grandfather, born in 1165
William R. Norwood – my great-grandfather
John Evan Norwood, Sr. – my grandfather
John Evan Norwood, Jr. – my father
John Vickers Norwood – Me

I promise, this is all going to get really exciting, but it needs some background. Hang in there with me.

The Norwood clan began in England, and through the generations, the Norwood name experienced several variations. Sir Stephen DeNorthwode was born in 1165 in Addington, an English village in the county of Kent. His great-grandson, John, changed the spelling to DeNorthwood, and for the next five generations the name was altered as follows:
Roger DeNorwood,
John DeNorthwood,
James Norwood,
John DeNorwood,
and John Norwood, my 14th great-grandfather.

The name remained Norwood for six more generations in England. It is interesting that each time my forefathers moved to a different town, they changed the spelling of their name.

Were my ancestors on the run from something or someone? Are there skeletons of notoriety in my ancestral closet?

Moving forward, my 8th great-grandfather, William Norwood, migrated from England to Surry County, Virginia where he married a Virginia lass in 1660. Their son, Edward, was the first Norwood born in America, in 1662. So, I am the 10th generation of Norwoods born in America.

"When does the exciting part kick in?" you ask.
It starts with Arabella.

My great-grandfather, William R. Norwood, born in Alabama in 1848, married **Arabella Jane Andress** in 1867, while they were both just 18 years old. They had six children, but three died in infancy. Their youngest, my grandfather, John Evan, was born in 1873, and shortly afterwards, the family moved to East Texas, making the long journey from Alabama by ox cart.

They settled in the Tempe community of East Texas, about eight miles out of Livingston, population 120, which was their nearest trading point and post office. William died in 1876 at the young age of 28.

Now here is an interesting fact. **My great-grandmother, Arabella Norwood, started the first Baptist Sunday School in the Tempe community of Polk County, Texas.** Arabella recorded some of her early memories in a notebook which she compiled from 1925-1929 while in her late 70's.

Here are some summaries from that notebook. I will put her direct quotes in italics.

14

After William's death, in 1876, my struggles began. *How and where to begin was one of the greatest problems of my life.* I farmed for one year, then the settlement offered me a position as teacher in the public school. Two communities combined and built a school house and a house for my family.

My salary was $15 a month. Of the 22 pupils, only six could read and write. Seven of the smaller ones had to live with my three children and me during the weekdays, because they lived too far away to walk home each afternoon.

I knew the most important thing for that community was the religion of Jesus Christ. There were four men and twelve women who professed to be Christians. At my suggestion, we found a preacher willing to come to our community once a week - a circuit riding Methodist preacher.

Next, I proposed we have a Sunday School, and we started on that first Sunday afternoon with 20 people of all ages. No one would step forward as the leader, so I reluctantly took the leadership.

Being a widow and a woman, I felt very incompetent, but *I realized it was the hand of God leading me. Oh, how I felt my weakness, but I did know that I was willing, so this thought came to me – God wants willing service, He can do the rest.*

Soon, some more Baptists, like me, moved to the community, and eventually we formed two churches - a Methodist and a Baptist.

Today as I write* (1928, at age 79), *while I have every comfort and all modern conveniences, I am not happier than I was in the days of my toil, hardships, and adversities. No, those were happier times… because we trusted God, looked on the bright side of everything, had a mind to work, and were grateful to our Heavenly Father.

I am so proud and grateful to have this heritage – a pioneer, church planting great-grandmother.

In 1884, eight years after William's death, Arabella married a Baptist minister, Rev. Thomas McCrorey, a widower with five children. He helped raise Arabella's three children, including my grandfather, John Evan. Thomas and Arabella had three more children. Thomas died in 1902, and Arabella never remarried. She died at the age of 82, in 1930.

My grandfather, John Evan Norwood, Sr., was injured as a child by a moving railroad engine, which caused him physical limitations the rest of his life. Converted under the preaching of his step-father in his early 20's, he was baptized at the Baptist church in Cold Springs. He met and married Leora Leggett in Livingston in 1899, and they had four sons – Leggett, who died at age six, Lloyd, Judson, and <u>my dad, John Evan Norwood, Jr.</u>

My grandfather was a member of the Masonic Lodge, as indicated by the symbol on his grave stone. He died in 1930, so I never met him. Leora remarried - to a Mr. Fain. I have not been able to find any of his background, and I do not remember ever knowing him. My grandmother, Leora, died in 1953.

So that's the story of how the Norwoods came to Livingston.

My Father

My dad, John Evan "Nib" Norwood, Jr, was born in Livingston on July 16, 1908, and never left Livingston, except for two years in college and the four years we all lived in Houston shortly after my birth.

His friends called him "Nib" or, sometimes, "Nubbins." You may wonder how he got that nick name. So did I. So did he. He simply said he had that nickname for as long as he could remember. It's even included in his name on his gravestone in Forest Hill Cemetery in Livingston, where he and Mom are buried.

Dad spent 13 years, from first grade through high school in one school building.

I asked him, "Why not just the normal 12 years?"

He said, "Well, I had so much fun in the third grade, that the teachers said I could stay there one more year."

That two-story school house was constructed in 1910 to contain all of the grades. Due to its mission-style architecture, people commonly called it **"The Alamo,"** which it resembled. I also attended The Alamo, for my six years of elementary school. They tore down The Alamo in 1981 to make way for newer buildings. That was sad for the old-timers, including Dad and me.

As a kid, Dad suffered two major accidents. The first one involved an encounter with a barbed-wire fence. Boys often wore knickers with knee-high wool socks. Attempting to crawl between two strands of a barbed-wire fence, he gashed his lower, left leg on a rusty barb. Unaware of the seriousness, he waited until the end of the day to examine it. The wound had absorbed the dye of the sock and soon became infected. As the infection got worse, the doctor said the leg might have to be amputated. Somehow, it healed in time, and the leg survived.

"Lookie here, son," he often said, showing me the grotesque scar on his leg as a vivid warning. "You watch yourself crossing them barb-war fences."

I was careful, indeed.

The other accident occurred in a car. A shattered windshield cut the tendon at the base of the middle finger on his right hand resulting in a dead finger that couldn't move. Being left-handed, he remained able to play sports, but the injury prevented his joining the military.

In high school, Dad excelled as a four-sport jock. He played end in football, first base in baseball, guard in basketball, and ran as a sprinter on the track team. If other sports were available, I'm sure he would have tried them.

After graduation from Livingston High in 1927, he and two friends got a football scholarship to Texas Military College in Terrell, Texas. Dad said that when they got off the bus in Terrell, they looked at each other and asked, "What in the world are we doing here?"

Dyke, who would remain a life-long friend, said, "I'm going back to Livingston," and got back on the bus. Terrell was too far from Livingston for him.

Dad stayed two years and graduated. Fortunately, it was a two-year junior college. I don't think he would have lasted four years.

He returned to Livingston and worked at one of the Sinclair gas stations managed by my uncle, A.E. Gerlach, who owned and managed Gerlach Brothers, the gasoline and oil supply warehouse for the Sinclair gas stations in Polk County. Dad was 30 years old and still unmarried - very unusual in those days.

Not to worry - the Lord had someone prepared for him.

My Mother

The scene changes to West Texas. My mom, Dorothy Brown Vickers, was born in Godley, Texas, a small farming town southwest of Ft. Worth, on April 22, 1911. The youngest of six, she had three brothers, Paul, Edwin, and I.T. Jr, and two sisters, Elizabeth, and Tommie. Yes, Tommie was her name, and everyone called her "Tom." I never thought anything about it until some of my college friends asked, "You had an aunt named Tom?" Yes, I did, and she was my favorite.

Mom's father, Isaac Thomas Vickers, born in Kentucky in 1865, came with his family to Texas in 1871 and settled in Johnson County, near Godley.

Her mother, Cora Lee Ryburn, was born in Mississippi in 1870. Apparently, her family also migrated to Texas, and Isaac and Cora were married in the early 1890's.

After five children, a 10-year interval occurred before Mom completed the family. **Possibly she was a surprise?** Usually, those kinds are spoiled, somewhat like an only child. The "only child" gets a lot of bad rap. I will discuss that later.

The Vickers were all good Baptists - pillars in the church and the community. Isaac Thomas, my grandfather, served as deacon in Godley Baptist Church for 51 years.

Besides siblings, Mom had cats. Stray cats, give-away cats, and natural born cats found a home at the Vickers' house. Her dad and brothers regularly found more suitable homes for the constant influx of felines. Sometimes Mom knew about it before-hand, but usually not. Her record was 17 cats at once. This probably happened after the brothers moved away from the homestead.

Mom's nickname was "Dot," from Dorothy. She excelled in grades and basketball. Being 5'9", and a good ball handler and shooter, she made the all-county team her senior year, 1928, at Godley High.

The next two years, she completed her freshman year of college at Baylor University and her sophomore year at Stephen F. Austin, where she joined the Pine Burrs, a service club on campus. Years later, she went to Livingston to live with her sister, Tommie, and Tommie's husband, August Edwin Gerlach, who happened to be my dad's boss.

That's where "Dot" met "Nib."

My Parents' Marriage (and their only child)

They didn't marry as teenagers or in their early twenties, as did several of their ancestors. Dad was 30, and Mom 27, when they married, on January 2, 1939. The newlyweds moved in with Dad's mother, Leora, and her second husband, Mr. Fain, in their rather large house. That must have worked out alright for almost three and one-half years - two old people and two not-so-young adults. Then I came along. **Things weren't very quiet and peaceful anymore.**

After my birth, my mom didn't like the unsanitary methods of Flowers' Hospital, so we only stayed a day and a half. We rode in an ambulance to our home, and were greeted by a practical nurse, and an aunt. My other grandmother and an aunt came two or three days later from Godley.

Grandmother Leora's large house had suddenly become very full of people. Seems I was high maintenance in the early days.

THE HOUSTON YEARS
1942-1947
Birth through Kindergarten

In July of 1942, six weeks after my birth, my parents and I moved to Houston. I'm not sure why we had to move so quickly, or so far away. Dad worked at Houston Shipbuilding Corp, making war ships - not models, the real ones. This was smack in the middle of the World War II years. He came home sometimes with his eyes burning from being around the welding. Later he worked for Eastern States Refining Company.

We lived in a small apartment in a lower-middle-class neighborhood. I had my own bedroom, and my first memories are of lying in a crib at age two or three. The paint on the head-board was cracking, and I liked rubbing my head against it getting my hair stuck so it would pull. Felt weird. I didn't have many toys to entertain me during the war years.

Another crib memory is of neighborhood kids - an older boy and girl - coming in to peek at me, thinking I was asleep. Apparently, they asked Mom to let them see the baby. They would exclaim, "Aw, how cute."

I hadn't yet developed my quick sense of humor, or I would have waited until they leaned-in for a closer look and jumped up screaming and lunging at them. That would have been a good laugh - at least once.

However, I didn't want to spoil a good thing, since they let me play out in the back yard with them. Mom trusted that we would all stay out of trouble - like exploring down the block, or playing out in the street, or injuring each other.

Our back yards were somewhat fenced in. The concern was to keep kids in, not to keep predators out. We were all so poor, no one would want to take us. Mom never worried about that. She explained to me years later, "If anyone ever did snatch you, they would bring you back pretty soon."

Seems I was a bit of a handful in my early years, if you want to believe the testimonies of my parents, doctors, teachers, relatives, neighbors, acquaintances and others who observed me from a distance. Thus, the backyard fence offered protection for those on both sides.

I do remember the uncontrollable urge to explore the front yard and the street as an adventurous three-year-old. Our side yard had a fence with a gate. When the world beyond the gate beckoned, I discovered some ways to undo the make-shift locks my parents rigged on the gate, and escaped to begin my exploration. I never got too far before Mom bolted out the front door, hysterically calling for me to "come back here right now." I figured she enjoyed the game as much as I did, so we often repeated it.

After a year or two, our parents trusted my friends and me out on the front sidewalk, where we engaged in my favorite activity - watercolors. One friend had a set of water colors and several tiny brushes. Early on, I demonstrated my lack of talent for art. Their pictures resembled animals, trees, houses, people - recognizable things. In my imagination, mine did too, but my friends lacked imagination.

"What's that blob supposed to be?" they asked.

They also accused me of mixing the colors and spoiling the jar of rinse water. Soon water-coloring ceased to be my favorite activity.

My lone memory of presents received during those lean years was a bicycle for my fourth birthday. Metal being purposed for war-equipment, bicycles were an unnecessary luxury. However, Dad somehow found a used bike, possibly one discarded as unusable, and made it rideable.

"What's that thing?" I asked when he brought it home.

"It's a bike, silly!" he explained.

It only slightly resembled a real bike, but it was my very own bike. I loved it. Dad helped me get started with my first few spills, and soon I could pedal it myself. I have always had good balance, and first demonstrated that ability by actually staying erect and propelling that bike down the sidewalk.

My friends laughed at my bike, but I knew they were just jealous. They were also smart enough not to try riding it themselves.

I don't remember us ever going to church in Houston, but Mom said we attended Park Place Baptist Church. I must have learned something about prayer, because my first prayer was for an apple tree.

In my bedroom, I had earned release from solitary confinement in my crib to my very own, very tiny, wooden bed with small mattress. Sitting in that bed, looking out the window, I longingly envisioned an apple tree growing right there in our side yard, and begged God for it. A reasonable request, I thought. I had a lot more to learn about prayer - and about where apple trees come from.

We had a cat named Greyboy. Mom simply had to have a cat. She let me name it, so I chose the name of the cat in one of my favorite nighttime story books.

"But this cat is a girl!", Mom argued.

"So?", I argued back. I won the argument, and we named her Greyboy.

Pre-kindergarten in Houston must have faded from my memory. My parents said that I went one year at Park Place Baptist Church, but I don't remember it. They said my teachers probably have a vivid memory of that year.

In November of 1947, I was five years old, and we moved back to Livingston. My parents must have missed Livingston, not to mention, hated Houston. We three were born to be country folks, not city folks. Greyboy, being a city cat, would just have to adjust.

WHAT WERE THINGS LIKE IN THE 1940s?

We are labeled "The Silent Generation" or "The Traditionalists" - born before "The Baby Boomers." I won't bore you with a lot of mind-boggling statistics and unbelievable facts...well, maybe just a few.

After researching my sketchy memory and the bottomless-pit internet, I've collected a few interesting details to amaze and inform you. All of this will relate only to American history and culture.

What things cost in 1945

First, let's list some average $ signs for the year 1945 - my third year of life. You should put "plus or minus" in front of each of these, meaning "somewhere around." (You can compare these to the 1950s on page 70.)

New house - $5,000
Rent - $40/month
New car - $1,000
Gas – 15¢ a gallon
Minimum wage – 40¢ an hour
Average annual income - $2,400
Member of US Congress salary - $12,500
Postage stamp – 3¢
One year tuition at Harvard - $420
Computer - $487,000 (but you needed 1800 square feet floor space to house it)

Inventions of 1940s

The 1940s gave us these cool inventions that are still in use today:

Aerosol spray can
Atomic bomb
Tupperware
Elmer's glue-all
Penicillin

Velcro
Slinky
Silly putty
Cheerios

Electric blanket
Duct tape
M&Ms
Scrabble

Slang of the 1940s

Every generation develops its own unique terms and phrases. Usually, youth are the innovators, and previous generations struggle to keep up. We old geezers have to ask our grandkids what modern expressions will make us cool/hip/groovy. Some of these 40s idioms are still in use today - and some are not.

Ace = person with a high level of expertise
Broad or dame = a woman
Chrome dome = a bald man
Cold fish or drip = a boring person, no fun
Wet rag/party pooper = same as above
A gas = a good time or something highly amusing
Dish = an attractive female
Dreamboat = a handsome male
Fat head, knuckle head = foolish person
Geezer = an old person
Above my pay grade = not in the know
Cut a rug = to dance
Decked out = dressed up nicely
Dope/scoop = information
Hot diggity dog = wow, yea
In cahoots = conspiring
Grandstand = to show off
Off the hook = found not guilty
Sweet = excellent

Bum rap = false accusation
Cockeyed = crazy, impossible
Crummy = no good
Crib notes = notes for cheating
Flip your wig = lose control, temper
Whistling dixie = wasting time
Rhubarb = a loud argument
Greenbacks = paper money
Pass the buck = blame someone else
Shut eye = sleep
Knuckle sandwich = a punch in the mouth
Old lady/man = mother/father
Cracks me up = makes me laugh
Swell = great

History of the 1940s

World War II characterized and shaped America in the 1940s. 1941-45 were years of grief, suffering, and untold violence. In 1945, the war ended in Europe on May 7 - V-E Day - after the defeat of Nazi Germany, and in Japan on August 14 - V-J Day - after the bombing of Hiroshima and Nagasaki. Sacrifice, and cooperation helped stop those oppressive regimes.

In 1947, The Red Scare, or McCarthyism began. Led by senator Joe McCarthy, this crusade against communism often made unfounded allegations of communist activity, resulting in paranoia. People wondered if their neighbors might be communist spies.

In 1948 the Cold War between the United States and Russia emerged, and people feared Russia would attack with atomic bombs. As a preschooler, I was blissfully unaware of these political and historical changes occurring all around me.

Culture of the 1940s, especially post-war culture

Post-WWII American culture went through many changes. Soldiers returned home, the marriage rate increased rapidly, and the Baby-Boom began. I am a pre-baby-boomer, but can still identify with that generation.
Radio maintained its popularity, but television loomed on the horizon. Rhythm and Blues of the 40s contributed to the development of Rock and Roll in the 50s.
In 1941, Ernest Tubb's "Walking the Floor Over You" launched the Honky-Tonk musical genre. A few years later, Hank Williams and others made it the predominant style in country music.
Music became more accessible with the introduction of the 33⅓ RPM record in 1948, and the 45 RPM record in 1949.
Several black athletes became popular heroes who paved the way for future generations. Joe Lewis reigned as heavy weight boxing champion from 1937-1949. Jackie Robinson became the first African American to play Major League Baseball in the modern era in 1947, and the first to be named Most Valuable Player in 1949.
Popular movie stars included John Wayne, Clark Gable, Bob Hope, Jimmy Stewart, Abbott and Costello, Ginger Rogers, Lana Turner, and Judy Garland. Popular movies, still remembered today, included: *Casablanca, It's a Wonderful Life,* and *Citizen Kane.*
Of course, my favorites were the "shoot-'em-ups." In those western movies you could tell the good guys from the bad by their cowboy hats - the good wore white, the bad wore black. The stories were clean and wholesome. Heroes shot the gun out of the villain's hand - never killed him. And they kissed their horses rather than wicked saloon women.
By the summer of 1945, Americans had been living under wartime rationing for more than three years. They were ready for a change. In fashion, "sporty and casual" replaced

"utility." The bikini swim suit debuted in 1946. Christian Dior launched the "New Look" in Paris, returning women's fashion to full skirts and feminine curves.

We three Norwoods, however, stuck to the utility look. I don't remember us ever being "in style." Maybe because of our financial situation, or more likely, because we lived in Poke County. And, by the way, Mom never wore a bikini.

In 1948 we were informed that the universe originated multiple billions of years ago with a Big Bang. Some folks forgot to check their Bible. That theory remains the same today - a theory.

Looking back, I remember that:

Kids respected and obeyed their parents.

Kids respected and obeyed their teachers.

Parents and teachers spanked kids.

People said "sir" and "ma'am" to their elders.

Kids played outside and improvised.

Divorce was rare. The nuclear family predominated.

Most stores were closed on Sundays due to Blue Laws, which prohibited the sale of certain products on Sunday.

Good families attended church.

Homosexuality was a taboo.

Pledge to the flag, Bible reading, and prayers in the classroom were common.

Want to learn more? Just watch some TV episodes of "The Andy Griffith Show," "The Waltons," and "Hogan's Heroes."

I have good memories of growing up in the 40s.

THE HIGHWAY 59 YEARS
1947-1950
Kindergarten through Second Grade

Returning to Livingston

We returned to Livingston in November 1947. Dad operated a Sinclair gas station until February 1948, when he took employment with Gerlach Brothers. Again, we lived with my grandmother, Leora, whose second husband, Mr. Fain, had passed while we were in Houston.

I remember really enjoying that house - plenty of room to run, and explore, and play cowboys and Indians, and hide from Dad and Mom and Grandmother. That didn't last long.

Grandmother owned a half block of property with three residences - her large house, a small garage apartment, and a small rent house. Soon we were moved out of the main house to the tiny apartment above the garage - not sure why. Apparently, that was also too close, so she moved us to the **small rent house, on Highway 59**, down the block, on the other side of her property. I don't remember seeing my grandmother a lot after that.

Our rent house, at the corner of Sherman and Highway 59, had a small kitchen, a tiny bathroom, and a front room which served as living room, dining room, and bedroom. We had close fellowship.

The perk for me was the front yard. I had a jungle for my playground on that corner. Actually, it was only one large oak tree, but I improvised. Dad hung a rope from one of the limbs. That became my Tarzan vine from which I swung around exploring the jungle and escaping apes and tigers.

For some unknown reason, my parents let me have a Jim Bowie knife. Jim's was huge - mine, a small replica. However, I became quite proficient at throwing my Bowie knife at my oak tree and making it stick.

For kindergarten we met in the teacher's house, across the street from The Alamo, my dad's old schoolhouse, which also served as my location of incarceration for six years. My only memory of kindergarten was my inability to use scissors. Maybe I preferred my Bowie knife, which I wasn't allowed to bring.

They cut our kindergarten experience short because most of the kids had mumps. Jimmy Glover and Mike Parker were the two classmates I remember. We three went through 12 years of school together and enrolled in the University of Texas together in 1960.

First-grade is something of a blur. I had a secret girlfriend, but she didn't know that until the eighth grade.

In general, I was shy and lacked confidence - probably because I was a bit small for my grade. Since I was born in late May, most of my classmates were older, some by six or seven months.

Many of my first-grade friends and I served 12 years together in Livingston schools and graduated together. Some of their names are ... OK, I deleted the rest of that sentence. I'm afraid I will hurt some feelings by leaving some out. Most of them, like me, can barely remember being in the first-grade anyway.

My parents - the Communists

My parents were Communists, or so I thought. They kept whispering secrets and discussing dark things when they thought I was asleep. I remember thinking something evil was going on, and my parents participated in it. I had heard about Communists - that they were our wicked enemies, and that some Americans actually spied for them.

This was during the McCarthy years, when Sen. Joseph McCarthy led a "witch-hunt" for Communists.

Could my parents actually be Communists?

Years later I found out that my dad was an alcoholic, and he would sometimes be drunk and uncontrollable. I remember one night Dad being loud and belligerent. His older brother, my uncle Judge, had come to our house to help Mom physically persuade him to get in my uncle's car.

I'm not sure where my uncle took him, but the next day Mom, Greyboy, and I were on a bus to Farmersville, northeast of Dallas, to stay awhile with her older sister, Beth. Roscoe and Beth Carlisle were gracious to keep us several times during those difficult years. When Dad sobered up, he would come to Farmersville and take us back to Livingston, until the next episode.

Sometimes he left the house for several days, and Mom told me he had to leave on business. During one of those periods, Mom instructed me not to go with him if he came to school to get me.

One night they discussed a separation, and Dad asked me which one of them I wanted to come live with. I loved them both and couldn't give him an answer. This was a sad time for me, during my impressionable sixth and seventh years.

Memories – Painful and Pleasant

Besides that source of frustration, my parents had another one to deal with - me. Seems I had some sort of condition of the nose and ear passages that required treatment.

"Treatment" in those years meant going to Houston to a doctor who would stick some pungent, stinging, gauze covered instrument up my nostrils and down my ear canals. It was torture. I screamed the whole time.

Mom and Dad told me years later, "You started screaming when we got in the car at Livingston for the two-hour trip to Houston."

Served them right for subjecting me to such agony, but I suppose it was for my own good.

Some of my favorite memories are the times I spent at Auntie's house. Edwin and Tommie Gerlach lived only four blocks away. Tommie was Mom's older sister, my "Auntie," and Edwin was Dad's boss at Gerlach Brothers.

Their daughters, Becky, 12 years older than me, and

Beth, 10 years older, were my favorite cousins, because they did fun stuff with me and spoiled me.

I loved spending Friday nights at their house. It was huge - three bedrooms, two baths, formal living room, formal dining room, large kitchen, and a combination family room and dining room. They were rich, and they owned something we couldn't afford - a radio.

Becky was away at college, so I slept in her room. When I woke up on Saturday mornings, I would go down the hall to Auntie's room, crawl under the covers, and turn on the radio while I waited for Auntie to serve my cinnamon toast. Yep, I was spoiled.

The radio was a table-top Zenith, about the size of an enormous bread box. Two or three hours passed quickly, listening to the thrilling adventures of Sergeant Preston of the Yukon (a Royal Mountie), Sky King (a pilot), and two of my favorite cowboys, Red Ryder and Roy Rogers.

Upon entering the second-grade at age seven, I joined the Cub Scouts, and scouting became one of the passions of my life. Cub Scout "campouts" meant taking an afternoon nap on blankets among the many trees in our den-mother's side yard. Years later, in Boy Scouts, we graduated to getting lost and spending spooky, nights in the wilds of the Big Thicket of East Texas.

All Cub Scouts entered the pack as Bobcats and worked their way up through the Wolf, Bear, and Lion ranks. I attained the rank of Webelos - an acronym for Wolf/Bear/Lion/Scout with vowels added. As a Cub Scout I earned a patch for each of those ranks and proudly graduated into Boy Scouts at age 11.

Spiritual Stirrings

Spiritual stirrings in my heart began during the first and second grades. Not many fun, sinful things were available, but, being human, I had the normal temptations to follow evil. One sin that nagged at my conscience for years was the time I "broke the law" and took my Colt 45 cap pistol to the movies.

The cap pistol, a realistic looking gun, contained a paper roll of exploding powder caps. With each pull of the trigger the hammer strikes the cap and produces a puff of smoke and the sound of gun fire. Of course, the cap guns were forbidden in movie theaters. Body checks and metal detectors weren't necessary, because there were always moms – the main deterrent.

My cousin, Becky, came home from college and planned to take me to a Lash LaRue cowboy movie one Saturday afternoon. Lash took down the bad guys using his only weapon - an 18-foot-long bull whip. Lash may need back up. I would be there for him - pistol in hand.

However, I had a dilemma. My cap pistol lay on a table close to the bed where my mom lay resting with a fever. How could I seize the pistol off the table and tuck it behind me, in my belt, under my shirt, and sneak it out of the house to the movie?

I devised a devious plan. Dad had washed dishes for Mom at noon before returning to work.

I approached her, "Hey Mom, come look at the funny way Dad hung the dish cloth in the sink."

It was the best I could come up with on short notice.

She replied, "I'm not feeling well, Johnny."

I insisted, "Aw come on, Mom, it's really funny."

After a few more pleadings, she relented and trudged into the kitchen for a quick glance.

"Yea, that's funny. Now get yourself ready. Becky will be here in a minute."

I stood ready, with cap pistol safely holstered behind me.

Becky and I arrived at the Fain, the only movie house in our small town at the time, and located a couple of seats that still had cushions on them. Fortunately, no incident occurred at The Fain that afternoon. When the lights went out for the movie, the cap gun came out, but not in Becky's sight, of course. Lash encountered trouble a couple of times, but didn't need my back up.

As I recall it now, the violation seems so minor, yet in my young mind, I had committed a major crime. I deceived my mother on her sick bed, and illegally sneaked my weapon into the theater. That sin haunted me for years.

Around that time, some of my friends at church presented themselves for baptism. I decided I wanted to be baptized, too, and often asked my folks about it. We had become active at Central Baptist Church, and I loved Sunday School.

At home, playing under my jungle tree, I practiced my evangelistic skills. I stopped people along the sidewalk and asked them if they "belonged to the church," as the expression went.

In the Spring Revival of 1950 at our church, I "came forward" and made my "profession of faith." Our pastor, Ben Welmaker, would soon leave for South America to become a missionary. The evangelist for the week, Vester Wolber, would replace him as pastor. The two reverends came to our house to talk with my parents and me.

All four were convinced I knew what I was doing, so I was baptized on April 21, 1950, at age seven. I must have been a good talker, because years later I realized I didn't really know what I was doing. There had been no real burden for and repentance from sin, and no significant change took place in my life.

There did seem to be a change in my parents' lives though, because Dad didn't have to go on "business trips" anymore, and Mom and I stopped rushing off to Farmersville.

That summer of 1950 we moved to a larger rent house, near the railroad tracks, and in September my parents "moved their letters" to Central Baptist. We were a happy family.

THE HOUSE BY THE TRACKS
1950-1952
3rd Grade through 4th Grade

Moving to the House By the Tracks

In the summer of 1950, after my release from second grade, we moved from the north edge of town to 507 Noblitt, on the south edge, all the way across town, a distance of less than a mile. Livingston was a very small town. Being barely eight years old, I don't remember anything about the actual move, but I liked the house and its location - there were woods just beyond my back yard.

The barbed wire fence, which separated our back yard and the unexplored forest, was insignificant to me. Of course, my parents instructed me not to cross that barrier. They warned that I might get lost in that wilderness full of snakes and boy-eating animals. Besides, they reasoned, it is illegal to enter someone's property beyond a fence, and our neighbors on the other side of the woods might be mean. I could hardly wait to crawl under that fence and begin my exploration.

That rent-house was a small, wood-frame, two-story, with a tiny kitchen and a medium-sized living room on the first floor. The second floor had a landing, bathroom, and bedroom. The landing, with a youth bed, served as my bedroom. The front door opened into the living room, and the back door led from the kitchen to the back yard. We felt like we were living in a mansion.

Across the street, some 100 feet from our mansion, were the railroad tracks. Trains came through town several times a day, and ours was the first house the engineer saw, signaling him to begin blowing his warning whistle.

"Whistle" hardly describes the piercing shrill that attacked our house and its occupants. After a few nights of jumping out of bed and under it to take cover, we got accustomed to the night time blasts. The day time ones were easier to take, because we could feel the rumble and hear the roar as the train approached.

A long stretch of blackberry vines filled the narrow area between our street and the railroad tracks. I loved picking and eating fresh blackberries. Sometimes I would pick a gallon or two for Mom to can.

However, caution was advised. If the vines had white, bubbly snake spit on them, a snake roamed the vicinity. Everyone knew this for a fact. Well, at least we kids knew it.

Somewhere up the ancestry line, a group of parents had concocted this "fact," presumably to scare their children and keep them away from possible snake locales. I reached adulthood before I learned the truth. The white foamy stuff came from spittlebugs.

Come to think of it, I'm glad I didn't know the true origin of the "snake spit." The blackberries tasted much more delicious, thinking I had looted them from the lairs of poisonous snakes.

One lonely, medium-sized tree stood in our front yard. It was about as tall as our house. Below the two upstairs windows, a narrow eave stretched the width of the house, and one of the tree limbs almost reached that eave.

It seemed conceivable to me that an eight-year-old boy could climb that tree, scoot out on the limb protruding toward the house, and nimbly transfer himself to the eave. Then he could open the window and enter the house.

I could hardly wait to run downstairs and surprise my folks, "Hey, bet y'all can't guess how I got into the house."

They would be pleased with my ingenuity and amazed at my dexterity.

First, I needed to make sure the feat was even possible, and decided to test my theory one afternoon. I climbed the tree with ease, but the limb assigned to bridge my connection to the house wasn't up to the task. It was long enough, but not strong enough. Within a foot of the eave, the limb cracked, and I went plummeting to the ground.

Next, I remember waking up on my bed. Dad sat there beside me. The haze slowly cleared, and I could see myself climbing that tree, inching out on the limb, but then all went blank.

I asked Dad, "Did I fall out of that tree?"

With a sigh of relief, he chuckled, "Yes, I heard the limb crack, and found you sprawled on the ground. You've been lying here in bed for several minutes."

I had no memory of the fall or of Dad carrying my limp body upstairs to the bed.

Mom was still out grocery shopping, so Dad and I made a covenant. First, I would never try that stupid trick again. Secondly, we would wait a long time before telling Mom what happened.

The Great Snake Hunt

My early forays into the woods beyond the backyard fence involved hunting for some of those snakes my parents warned me about. My parents were slow to learn that warnings constitute challenges.

Unaware of my intention to go snake hunting, Dad helped me make a neat set of bow and arrows. A green, limber tree branch, about one-half inch thick, formed the bow, with thin twine for the bowstring.

The arrows were much thinner, somewhat straight, branches. The tips of the arrows were sharpened on one end, and folded cardboard strips served as feathers on the other end. Dad set up a cardboard box as the intended target. Several strategically placed arrow holes in the box assured my parents I knew how to use my toy in the proper manner.

One afternoon I got my chance to go look for a snake. To my surprise, not far inside the forbidden territory, I met a snake, all curled up taking a nap. I kept my distance and launched a few arrows in his direction. He didn't move.

Probably because none of the arrows came even close. I inched forward - twang, twang, twang. The snake raised his head and lazily peered at me.

Being out of arrows, I had to circle around the snake to retrieve them. Meanwhile, the snake became mildly interested in the situation and stretched to its full 18-inch length.

Knowing my window of opportunity was quickly closing, I stepped within three feet and shot an arrow straight down at him. Thunk! The arrow hit the snake and bounced off. He glared at me menacingly, and slithered into the underbrush.

Disappointed, I picked up the arrow and then observed - there was blood on the tip! I had actually shot a snake with my bow and arrow.

Rushing back through the woods, under the fence, and into the house, I proudly displayed the bloody arrow and announced to my parents, "I just shot a snake!"

Dad looked up from his newspaper and said, "Oh, really? Well, leave it out in the yard."

Dads generally don't over-react. Moms do, though.

"You what? Where were…did it…where is… why were… how did…," she sputtered frantically.

Finally, she calmed down, and I explained I had only nicked the snake, and it crawled away. The usual reprimands and warnings ensued, but I was used to them, and it was worth it. I had shot a snake.

The following day at school, the snake miraculously increased in size, as did the amount of blood shed. The story morphed into a safari-type epic adventure. My friends were awed that I had bravely stalked and mortally wounded a giant python with nothing more than a home-made bow and arrow.

I kept that arrow, with the drop of blood on the tip, safely hidden, out of sight, under my bed. No sense in letting it ruin a good story.

The Long, Long Tunnel

It was an ingenious idea. The tunnel would stretch from my house to Mack's. We could secretly visit each other via the tunnel anytime we wanted. My best friend, Mack Porterhouse, and I lived almost two miles apart, on opposite sides of town. Eight-year-old boys usually don't make that long a trip on their bicycles alone. Well, we had done it a time or two, but our parents never knew it.

So, finally we had a project that wouldn't fail. Previous inspirations always sounded good when we dreamed them up, but, so far, none of them had fulfilled their promise. This one would though. It was fool proof.

We decided to begin the tunnel at my house thinking the direction would be north to south, which obviously is downhill. This would make the digging easier. Years later we realized our miscalculation. Mack's house was north of mine, not south. Possibly that's the reason the project proved to be so difficult.

We had chosen a spot in my side yard, right next to the street. This way passers-by could observe and marvel at our tunnel.

Ground breaking day arrived. It had been delayed a few days because Mack couldn't think of an acceptable way to convince his parents that he needed to bring their shovel to my house. We discussed several possibilities - we need to bury my dog, or we need to dig for worms, or we're looking for hidden treasure.

Mack's parents were stricter than mine and less gullible. We ditched all those ideas, and Mack simply sneaked out of the house that day bringing the shovel on his bike. He figured he could deal with the consequences later.

It was 9:00 o'clock in the morning, so we had all day to dig. Surely, we could get half way to Mack's house and finish the tunnel the next day. Armadillos could dig several times their length in minutes. Why couldn't we? We began to dig.

Mack went first, since it was his shovel. Placing the shovel on the spot we had marked "X," and his foot on the shovel, Mike applied the full weight of his hefty body. Nothing happened. The "X" was still there. The shovel was still poised on the surface of the ground. Mack tried jumping up and down on the shovel. Still nothing. This undertaking might be slightly more problematic than we anticipated.

Eight-year-old boys are easily discouraged, so we needed something positive to happen. Mack was both the brains and the brawn of this excavation team. Brilliantly, he laid the shovel flat on the ground and scraped it forward, producing a half-inch layer of dirt on the shovel. The "X" disappeared! Triumphantly, he threw the shovel-load of dirt over his shoulder. We were on our way to his house now!

After a few more scrapings and tossings, I took over the digging. Gripping the shovel, I mused, *This thing, unlike me, is really big - and heavy.* But I didn't say that to Mack, who had handled it like a toy. Tentatively, I poked at the ground with the point of the shovel. That ground was solid!

I raised the shovel some two feet above the ground and rammed it downward with all my might. The shovel dug in. All of a sudden, we witnessed a lot of screaming and leaping. The shovel had hit my big toe.

I did a magnificent imitation of a ballerina - grasping the injured toe, pointing the leg straight up in a vertical position and bounding around the tunnel site on the other leg. I yelled out every expletive I knew - which at my age were only a few and very mild. Mack rolled on the ground in fits of laughter. Later in life that incident became humorous for me too - much later.

It took a while for me to walk normally again, and for Mack's frequent fits of laughter to subside, but eventually we got back to serious digging. Mack did most of the productive work while I continued to provide comic relief by my ineptitude at plying a shovel. We had reached a depth of some three inches by noon. Time for lunch and a much-deserved break.

Both of my parents worked, so we had the house to ourselves. After a quick sandwich and soda water we returned immediately to our task - right after looking at a couple of my newest comic books and playing a few hands of "Battle" and "Go Fish."

Mysteriously, the afternoon had slipped away, and my parents would be home in a couple of hours. We rushed back to our project, which by now we realized might take more than two days.

Feverishly, we scraped, poked, and swore at the stubborn hole in the ground. It was now about three feet wide and four inches deep. We had a long way to go. Five p.m. approached - time for my parents to get home, and time for Mack to hustle back home with his shovel and face the consequences. I didn't envy him.

We needed to abandon the tunnel for today - maybe for several days - but not forever. We would never admit defeat.

Actually, we never got back to the project. It lay dormant for months, unnoticed by anyone and totally forgotten, until one afternoon, Dad and I were clearing the side yard of some weeds and vines.

Dad noticed a slight indentation in the ground and asked, "What's this little sink-hole doing in the ground?"

"Hmmmm, I have no idea," I lied.

No need to concern him with the original purpose of that indentation. He would probably tell Mom, and they would worry about us traveling back and forth through the tunnel when we finally finished it. Parents are like that.

The Disastrous Duet

Our third-grade teacher, Miss Evila Hartless, announced her brilliant idea. The class would pair up and sing duets the next day, as a climax to the week of music education. The girls loved the idea. The boys had a different opinion. Quickly, the pairs formed, and only two boys remained unclaimed, like two non-descript stubs of crayons in a box of new ones – Lester Bright and me.

We called him Less Bright, which described his mental capacity. Less wasn't playing with a full bag of marbles. Poor guy could hardly read or write. After repeating first-grade several times, he got a free pass each year through junior high just to keep him in school.

Less did have one moment of glory, years later, in the seventh-grade. The math teacher attacked us with a dreaded "pop-quiz," giving us a single problem to solve, and it was a toughie. We struggled with it until forced to submit our written answers.

The teacher looked at our random guesses and read them aloud, declaring each one wrong. Then he read the final one - Less's. Less had written the number he only recently learned to write - "100." That was the correct answer! We cheered Less, and he beamed with pride.

In our class, Less towered above all of us - a third-grader in a sixth-grade body. My major concern for the impending choral finale was Less' inability to sing, which matched my own skill level. Neither one of us could carry a tune in a bucket. This was going to be the "Disastrous Duet." I desperately needed an excuse for missing school.

The next morning, I woke up and declared, "I'm too sick to go to school today."

Mom retorted, "No you're not. Get up and get dressed."

I shouldn't have told her last night what loomed ahead.

"But my throat is sore. I can't sing," I rasped.

"Voice sounded OK when you said you were sick." Moms are hard to fool. After breakfast, I tried again. "My bike has a flat. I'll be late." Dad waited at the door. "Come on and get in the truck. I'll take you to school on my way to work." Dad and I examined my bike. Strangely, the flat tire had revived and was full of air, so I reluctantly allowed it to transport me to school.

Thus, I found myself sitting at my desk, in a cold sweat, awaiting the approaching calamity. The pairs of vocalists were to prepare a song of their choice. Several magnificent performances impressed and entertained us. Even some boys demonstrated surprising potential in singing.

The teacher had cruelly saved our fiasco for last. "Alright, Lester and Johnny, it's your turn."

We trudged toward the front hoping for a miracle. Maybe the recess bell would malfunction and ring early. Maybe the teacher would have pity and tell us to just sit back down. Maybe the Principal would surprise us with a Fire Drill. Maybe Jesus would return. All of these were far more likely to happen than the one miracle we silently prayed for - to be able to sing a recognizable song.

Arriving at the front, we turned like condemned criminals, to face our executioners, who were, with difficulty, restraining their snickers and jeers. We resembled the popular comic strip characters, Mutt and Jeff - one too tall and one too short.

Suddenly, Less and I looked at each other in panic, realizing we had not discussed what to sing. An inspiration hit me, and I whispered, "OK, Less, let's try singing 'Happy Birthday' to the class. I'll start us off, you follow along."

To the onlookers I announced, "Less and I dedicate this song to each of you - our classmates."

"Happy Birthday to you..." I began, and Less squawked right along with me. We produced terrible two-part disharmony, but everyone loved it.

For the closing line, we magnanimously stretched out our arms and screeched in loud disunity, "Happy Birthday, dear Claaaaass, Happy Birthday to you."

Laughing, clapping, and cheering erupted. The miracle we prayed for had happened.

My Dog Butch

We still had our aging cat, Greyboy, but I wanted a dog. Every boy needs a dog. Actually, I would have settled for a brother or even (gag) a sister. All my friends had one or more. At least a sibling would be younger, thus raising my status in the family. But the prospects didn't seem likely, so I needed to campaign for a dog.

Mom was a cat person, and Dad's only experience with animals, in his growing up years, was to shoot and eat them. What could I do to convince them we needed a dog? Whine? Plead? Bargain? Threaten?

The combination succeeded. After I agreed to feed and bathe the dog, they relented. Soon, Dad brought home a cute, fuzzy, Heinz-57 puppy. He grew to be a medium-haired "Golden Cocker Beagle" - one of a kind. We named him Butch. Before long he won our hearts.

Butch joined the family on a Saturday. Sunday morning, I asked Mom and Dad if we could stay home from church, so I could take care of Butch.

I explained to them, "Butch, being still in infantile puppy stage, will assuredly have the proclivity towards horrendous apprehension and perplexity if compelled to endure solitary confinement."

At least that is what I attempted to express to them, if not in those exact words.

What my parents heard was "Pleeeeeeeeeeease!!" in a whiney, sobbing wail. It worked. We stayed home, and I sat on the floor most of the day, holding Butch in my lap. Boy and dog formed a bond that day which would last for 12 years.

Greyboy had a different perspective, though. She had been top cat for eight years, and was not about to give up that position to a disgusting little ball of fur. She often reminded Butch of the pecking order with a spiteful hiss or a well-placed claw. Theirs became a love-hate relationship of tolerance.

However, one day, two-year-old Butch became very sick. He could hardly move, and preferred to lie out in the back yard alone, not really wanting any petting or food or water. Greyboy, with her motherly instincts, volunteered to nurse Butch back to health. She spent most of two days lying beside him, without saying a word. The next day Butch recovered, and Greyboy resumed her "I can't stand you" attitude toward him.

Butch went with me everywhere, which included some places neither one of us should be going. Hey, a boy and his faithful dog have to be given some freedom to explore. Sometimes I rode my bike, sometimes we were both afoot, but always together.

As for tricks, Butch had a rather sparse resume'. He did learn to fetch a thrown stick. His problem was his owners. We didn't know how to teach a dog to do tricks. I am sure he could have been a great performer if only given the proper training.

He proved this to be true years later, after we had moved to our next house on Calhoun Street. Butch noticed that every Sunday, we got in the car and left him at home alone all morning with Greyboy. Neither of them liked this arrangement, so Butch decided to do something about it.

Early on, we had disciplined him not to follow the car when it left the house, and he obeyed. However, for several Sundays, we noticed that when we left for church, and the car was almost out of sight, Butch raced up the road behind us.

Of course, he couldn't keep up with the speed of the car, but each Sunday he followed a little bit farther.

One Sunday after church, we walked to the side street where we had parked in our usual spot and noticed something under the car - it was Butch! Somehow, he followed our trail to church, located our car, and waited for us, sheltered comfortably from the sun like a sentry, waiting for his masters. We rewarded him for his ingenuity with a ride home in the car.

The next Sunday, as we were dressing for church, Butch was nowhere to be found. That seemed strange. He always took the opportunity to mope around and give us his "pitiful me" look that said, *Are you really going to leave me alone again with that dreadful cat?* We went on to church, knowing Butch would greet us heartily when we got home.

What a surprise awaited us! As we pulled up to park in our usual spot at church, there was Butch, lying on the pavement, eagerly anticipating our arrival. He had left the house early, so he could reserve our usual parking place for us.

Our route between house and church was via highway and paved roads. Butch's route, was "as the crow flies," or in his case, "as the dog weaves," through yards and fields and dirt roads - about one mile in distance.

In the weeks that followed, Butch became well known as a faithful attender of Central Baptist Church. Besides making a great story, we got an added bonus - we never had to worry about someone taking our parking spot.

Last Chosen

Baseball was my first love - an unrequited love during my elementary school years. I could handle girls snubbing my amorous affections, but why did baseball so callously reject my devotion? I adored her, but she spurned my every attempt to form a relationship. It was a one-sided love affair.

After school and during the summers, we guys played baseball. On the grade-school playground, however, the girls joined in, so we played softball to avoid injuries. Some of my most embarrassing moments occurred when it came time to choose teams for softball. I can still replay those scenes in my memory's VCR.

"OK kids, today you're playing softball," the recess supervisor announces. "Everyone that wants to play, gather round."

We come running, eager to play - mostly boys and some girls. Two players are assigned as captains with the privilege of choosing teams. They stand facing the lineup of potential players and survey the prospects.

We hopefuls line up like volunteers to be auctioned to the highest bidder. One by one, the line reduces to one remaining player - me. Even the girls are chosen before me - very humiliating.

"Alright, let's play some softball," the captains shout, as one team scatters to the field, and the other prepares to bat.

Then someone sees me standing alone with drooped shoulders, and yells, "Hey, wait, Norwood hasn't been chosen yet."

"You take him," one captain says.

"Nah, I chose last. He's yours," the other retorts.

Knowing my usual field assignment, I head to the far corner of right field, where few balls are hit.

When we are "in town," our turn to hit, I am the last in the batting order. If there are already two outs when I come up to bat, my teammates moan, grab their gloves, and head toward the field, as I stand there at the plate. They know the third out is coming - and it usually does.

At least, I did hit the ball every time, never striking out. Good eye-hand coordination was one of my rare athletic abilities. The power just wasn't there.

My weak grounders looked like lethargic frogs hopping into the fielder's glove, and my infield pop-ups like descending butterflies waiting to be snared. Yep, I was a scrawny weakling in those days. Very embarrassing.

Those were my elementary school years. In high school, however, things changed. My baseball career began to blossom. Those stories will come later. Thankfully, I was no longer last chosen.

Paper Boxes

Fourth-grade boys are mischievous - my friends and I being prime examples. Now you have to understand that some 10-year-old boys in my class were downright mean and destructive. They put live garter snakes in kids' lunch boxes, dipped girl's pigtails in inkwells, and shot innocent birds and unsuspecting people with their slingshots. My cohorts and I, on the other hand, were simply full of harmless mischief.

Several of our favorite activities, to relieve the boredom of school work, involved making small paper boxes. Whoever invented the folded paper box was a genius - obviously not from my group of friends.

You start with a square piece of paper, eight by eight inches, which is easily made by folding and tearing off three inches from the bottom of a standard sheet of writing paper. Several folds and tucks later you have a flat six-sided figure with a slight opening at one corner.

Next comes the magic. While lightly grasping the paper form, with a flourish you blow a quick, firm puff of air into the opening and - Presto! You have a hollow, two-inch, paper cube. The box is fully closed except for the top side, which has a small opening. Widen this hole to accommodate the objects you want to insert in the box.

Girls liked to make these paper boxes and decorate them with crayon designs, pictures, and writing. The really wicked girls connived to snatch an unsuspecting boy's paper box, decorate it all girlie-like, and sneak it back on his desk.

"Hey, who's been messing with my paper box?" he snarled, holding the box up for all to see. He should have kept quiet and hidden it. But it was too late.

Some guy nearby announced, "Whoa, everyone, look at Johnny's paper box. He made it all girlified." The whole class, including the teacher, focused on the gaudy box and exploded in laughter.

News like this traveled fast at the Alamo. By recess, everyone had heard. Although the box now lay dead in the wastebasket, torn to shreds, the story was alive and growing - all over the playground.

"Did you hear that Johnny is making colorful, dainty paper boxes for everyone?" the boys tormented.

"Oh, Johnny, how sweet. Make me one pleeeeeease," the girls teased.

Already having a low self-esteem, this was not the kind of popularity I longed for. After that, I kept my paper boxes secure and reserved to fulfill their two intended purposes - jails and bombs.

The "jail-box" served to incarcerate flies which we boys captured live. There are two ways to catch a fly without squishing it into a bloody mess.

The easiest method is to wait for it to land and immediately clap cupped hands a few inches above the fly. Flies generally panic at the sudden movement and zoom straight up into the cupped hands. The percussion of the clapped hands stuns the fly, and it spirals down to its original spot in a daze. Gingerly pick up the fly and imprison it in your jail-box before it revives and begins its mad attempt to escape.

The most impressive method of apprehending flies is to nab them with one hand in mid-flight. That's not easy and takes much practice. You also run the risk of getting fly mush all over your hand.

"Why capture flies and put them in paper jail-boxes?" one might ask. Obviously, that person never experienced the thrill of chasing girls around the playground with a paper box full of angry, loud-buzzing, wing-flapping flies. Hilarious for the boys. Gross for the girls.

Secondly, the paper box functioned as a waterbomb-box. One day a couple of ill-behaved boys, Fibber Odis Gusting and his friend, filled their paper boxes with water and hurried to the second-story window of the Alamo, which overlooked the side-door exit below. They readied their waterbombs and waited for some girls to appear, heading outside for recess.

When a waterbomb box hits the sidewalk at the target's feet, there is a glorious splash of water, drenching the victim. Of course, a bull's eye, landing splat on top of the head, is even more satisfying.

This was not the first time these and other boys had attempted bombing raids on unsuspecting girls. After a successful blitz, girls cautiously reconnoiter the windows above the exits for days. Thus, this duo of attackers waited until suspicion had waned. Another bombardment was due - that day.

Like World War II bombardiers, they perched at the window sill with a loaded waterbomb in each hand, scanning the landscape below for the enemy. Timing is the key. They must listen for girls' voices, ascertain their location, and judge the timing for the release of the bombs.

Waiting for the girls to appear, then heaving the bombs at them, was not an option. These bombs were fragile, already beginning to leak water, and threatening to detonate at any moment. A thrown water bomb could blow up prematurely in the launcher's hand. It was all guess work that required skill and experience, neither of which these two assailants possessed.

"Listen, Fibber, some girls are really close," the other boy whispered evilly.

"Wait 'til I give the signal. I'll nudge your arm, and we'll drop the bombs," Fibber instructed.

The giggly voices approached unaware of the impending doom. Suddenly, Fibber nudged his friend's arm - time for "bombs away." Four already dripping water bombs descended on the enemy. Kersplash! It was a perfectly timed, pinpoint explosion - except for one minor miscalculation. A silent teacher, one step in front of the chattering girls, shielded them and received the full impact of the barrage.

Mrs. Gauntletson screamed and fumed like a scalded dragon. The girls behind her froze in horror. Heads were going to roll, for sure.

Terror stricken, Fibber and his accomplice vanished in a flash and instantly reappeared on the playground, quickly mingling among the other kids. An intensive inquisition followed, but, with no eyewitnesses, except the guilty two, no heads rolled. Fortunately, finger printing, security cameras, and lie detectors were not yet available at Livingston Elementary School.

More waterbomb attacks were launched in the years to follow, but not by Fibber and his friend. One narrow escape from life imprisonment was enough for us.

Small-Town Entertainment

Everyone knew everyone in Livingston. With a population somewhere under 2800, if a new-comer showed up, everybody knew it. Small businesses were locally owned and operated, so the "chain stores" went elsewhere to look for bigger markets. Our economy was built on lumber, farming, some ranching, and those small businesses. We were rural East Texas.

For entertainment we had two movie theaters - The Fain, and another smaller theater that lasted only a few years. The historic Fain Theater, built in 1940, entertained patrons until June 2015 as one of the longest running theaters in Texas history.

A "cry room" in the back provided a sound proof room for moms with small children. Thankfully, I never had to be taken there. Segregation being the law of the land, black and white movie-goers purchased tickets at separate booths and even sat separately.

The Fain put out a monthly schedule of upcoming movies. Printed on letter-size cardstock in two colors, it had a tiny billboard type picture of the actors and action of each movie. These were collector's items, although we didn't realize it at the time. Just for the fun of it, I saved those posters for several years. Sadly, today I have no idea what happened to that marvelous collection.

The movie ticket price gradually went from 15 cents to 30 cents during my early years of movie going. Another 15-30 cents would buy you a Coke, a candy bar, and a small bag of popcorn. Yes, each item could be purchased for a nickel, and gradually went up to a dime.

Week nights had two showings, but Saturdays played the movie from morning to evening. You could pay once and stay all day. My friend, Mardan Raunchy, and I sat and watched a Roy Rogers movie four times one Saturday.

Another great entertainment was Friday Night Calf Roping, held in the rodeo arena at the Polk County Fairgrounds, just south of town. Cowboys competed in ... well, calf roping.

Pumped-up cowboy on horse and frightened calf in escape-mode are released from adjacent chutes, and the race against time begins. The cowboy's objective is to lasso the calf, dismount, throw the calf on its side, and tie three legs together with a six-foot cord in as short a time as possible.

The calves are not hurt in this event, but they certainly aren't happy either. The quick and skillful roping, throwing, and tying of a calf is very impressive and entertaining.

But just as entertaining, for its hilarity, is the struggle of a frustrated cowboy with a calf that refuses to be thrown on its side. In a flurry of flailing hoofs and tangled rope, exasperated cowboy and bellowing calf "fight for their lives" amidst a cloud of dust. Humiliating for the cowboy. Satisfying for the calf.

For those who couldn't afford the price for movies or calf roping, there was fire practice. The local fire department had to keep their skills sharp, so they often conducted fire practice. The firetruck parks near a fire hydrant in town, and firemen hustle to connect the hose and spray water full-blast down a vacant street.

This occurred rather late at night to avoid hitting vehicles or pedestrians. Very entertaining in our small town, and well attended. Small town entertainment was generally unique and cheap.

In our first year of marriage, my wife, Diana, and I visited her parents in Dallas. They took us for a late-night drive downtown to "see the lights." We saw a street flowing with water, which obviously shouldn't be there.

I commented, "They must be having fire practice."

After an awkward pause and silence, Diana asked, "What do you mean, fire practice?"

"The fire department must be out practicing with their fire hoses," I explained.

Surely these big-city folks could understand that. The more I explained the more they laughed. Sadly, these people had never experienced the thrill of watching fire practice.

At the end of the street, we saw a broken water line spewing water. Repairmen would soon be there to stop the flow down the street. It would be much later before the flow of laughter stopped in the car.

High school football, basketball, and baseball games were another great form of inexpensive entertainment. Admission was cheap, and the Cokes, candy, and popcorn only cost you 5-cents each.

My friends and I liked the football games best. The football field lay inside the oval-shaped 440-yard cinder track used for track meets. Two sets of bleachers bordered each side of the field and track - one set for home team fans, and a smaller set for the visitors.

We kids never sat on the bleachers. To watch the game, we joined a throng of spectators who moved up and down the cinder track to follow the progress of the football. A three-foot high chain-link fence separated us from the field and our team's bench. We liked to be close to the action.

When the game got boring, we youngsters improvised a football game of our own in one of the endzones. Several discarded drink cups stacked together make a usable, if not so aerodynamic, football.

Teams were chosen, and the game proceeded, until interrupted by the main football game. If the fans' yelling alerted us that the home team was doing good, we called time-out and watched for a few minutes. Also, if a team was about to score at our endzone, the referees blew their whistles and yelled at us to vacate the field.

Baseball games were also fun. Our favorite part was chasing foul balls that flew over the stands behind home plate and landed in the dirt parking lot. A mad rush ensued, as a dozen or so kids chased the rolling baseball between, under, or on top of the cars.

Foul balls down the right field or left field lines landed in the woods. These were harder to find, but just as rewarding. The lucky kid that retrieved the ball and returned it to the concession stand got a free soda water. A nickel earned is a nickel saved.

Holidays were chock-full of fun for everyone in our small town, but I will give you the kids' perspective - mainly, we got out of school.

Thanksgiving meant turkey, pecan pie, and football. Before having TVs to view football, we had to make do with the real thing. Many families had a traditional touch football game in the yard. Participants were young and old, male and female, family and friends - whoever happened to be there.

Christmas meant presents - and more turkey. The Christmas and New Year's break gave us two full, glorious weeks of vacation. However, change of semester occurred mid-January, and for high school and college students, the dread of semester finals was a fly in the ointment for Christmas break.

New Year's and July 4th meant firecrackers. I was an avid popper until New Year's Eve of 1953. I mischievously broke off a length of fuse from a Baby Giant, intending to light it, throw it at a friend's feet, and yell, "Baby Giant." I mistakenly lit the short fuse of the firecracker itself and woke up in the hospital. The explosion had mangled my hand and temporarily deafened my friend who was crouching in front of me, ear-level with the Baby Giant. That was the last firecracker I ever popped.

Halloween meant candy. Disguised as an assortment of monsters, we canvassed the neighborhoods "trick or treating" for goodies to fill our large paper bags which we got from the grocery store. In those days we went out in small groups of friends (no parents allowed), and stayed out late.

"What about television?" you may ask.

Well, we had heard of it in the late 1940's, but very few families owned one. Uncle Edwin and Aunt Tommie were the first in our family to buy one. Theirs was huge - the size of a large chest-o-drawers. However, the screen measured only about 12 inches diagonally. This made for intimate family fellowship, because you had to gather really close to see the picture.

When the screens increased in size in the early 1950's, our local John Deere tractor store bought a TV and placed it in the front showroom window, next to the sidewalk and street. On Friday nights they showed professional wrestling from Houston's City Auditorium.

Mom, Dad, and I arrived early so we could park Dad's pickup at the curb, facing the television - especially during the winter. In warmer weather, we might join the crowd sitting on the sidewalk to get a closer view.

Some of our favorite wrestlers were:

"Killer" Kowalski – a 6-foot 7-inch, 290-pound giant, who developed a "villain" persona.

"Wild Bull" Curry – who looked and acted like a wild-man with his bushy eyebrows, maniacal facial expressions, and un-predictable violence.

Danny McShain – who often cut his own forehead during matches to draw blood, and used the "piledriver" move, holding his opponent upside-down and dropping him head-first onto the mat.

Gorgeous George – who sported golden locks, draped himself in lace and fur, and entered the ring to the music of "Pomp and Circumstance."

No one ever considered that some of their antics might be only theatrics. We were eyewitnesses to the groans and the body slams and the blood. This was real and serious, with nothing "fake" about it - wholesome competition and fine entertainment.

As I said before - small town entertainment was generally unique and cheap.

The Whuppin'

We lived in the house by the tracks during my third and fourth years of confinement in The Alamo. I didn't really resent school too much, because my friends were there with me. Misery loves company.

My teachers were nice, and I only got one paddling, although I probably deserved many more. I just had a knack for not getting caught. Corporal punishment in those days was expected and effective. Almost every day, some miscreant got a "whuppin."

My whuppin' was worth the pain. One day, our second-grade teacher, Mrs. Willowbranch, called Grubby Brackish to the front to write on the chalk board. Grubby was a fat, obnoxious bully and very unpopular.

As he pranced up the aisle past my desk, I jabbed my foot out to trip him. He fell splat, face-first on the floor with a thud and loud scream. David had toppled Goliath. The class burst into cheers, and I became an instant hero.

The laughter continued as Grubby gathered himself up, trying to regain some dignity. I noticed Mrs. Willowbranch trying her best to stifle a chuckle as she called for order in the classroom.

Summoning Grubby to her desk, she interrogated him, "What do you think you're doing, showing off like that?"

"It was Norwood. He tripped me," he pleaded.

Managing a look of shock and innocence, I explained, "I was just stretching my leg." It was true, if not the whole truth.

"Johnny, you come up here, too," she barked.

I hustled up front to join Grubby. He hoped for retribution. I was basking in the affirmation of my classmates. The teacher flung open her desk drawer and, with a flourish, withdrew the dreaded wooden paddle, like a knight dramatically brandishing her sword. There was a collective gasp, then silence.

"Grubby, bend over my desk," she instructed. Grubby bent over the desk. This was going to be great. He was tough, but on the third whack to the seat of his pants, Grubby emitted a slight whimper. More cheers and laughter.

The fourth whack broke the paddle in half. Suddenly - a ray of hope for me. Maybe the teacher didn't have a back-up paddle.

However, teachers are resourceful, not to mention sinister. She ordered me to bend over the desk, and administered my four whacks with a doubled paddle, using both pieces.

The resounding clack of the paddle pieces against my posterior brought more gasps from the on-lookers. Strangely, however, it hardly hurt. Was it the exhilaration of my achievement, or could Mrs. Willowbranch have actually dialed back the intensity? Either way, it was a double win for me. I had humiliated the class bully, and I had not whimpered during our punishment.

Another thing about "whuppings" in that day - if you got one in school, you got one back home. Case closed.

Mom picked me up in her car after school. I knew she would eventually hear about my paddling, so figured I might as well get it over with. I told her what happened.

Up to this point in my upbringing, Mom and Dad had never given me a spanking - some rather stern reprimands, but never a spanking. We discussed the situation on the way home. It was not clear yet which parent would administer the punishment, but I was already suffering in trepidation.

Mom had been grocery shopping, so I offered to help bring in the groceries, hoping to have my sentence commuted to time served, if not altogether pardoned. With a double-arm-load of groceries Mom swung her hip against the car door to close it, not realizing that I was reaching for one remaining item in the car seat. I jerked my arm away, but not fast enough. The door slammed on my thumb and I screamed in agony.

Clutching my bleeding, opposable digit in the other hand, I danced around the vicinity whooping and crying. Mom was horror-stricken and joined in the screaming and dancing. She had wounded her only child. Ah-ha! Opportunity had presented itself, and I must seize the moment. Submissively, I let her rush me into the house to "doctor" my swelling, bleeding thumb.

"Doctoring" in our home was fairly simple, consisting of only three medications, depending on the nature of the ailment.

If it itches, use Calamine Lotion. It's somewhat soothing, but messy when applied, and flakey when it dries.

If it hurts inside, use Milk of Magnesia. It's intended to soothe the lining of a sick tummy, but it tastes horrible and always made me throw up.

If it is bleeding, use Mercurochrome. It's a red antiseptic, alleged to facilitate healing. It was like pouring dark red alcohol on an open wound and hurt worse than the original injury. Dad jokingly called it "monkey blood."

For example, one day he noticed some blood on my arm and called out to Mom, "Hey, Kid (his pet nickname for her), bring me the monkey-blood. Johnny's got a scratch on his arm."

Mom rushed to the scene, looking concerned, "OK, here's the Mercurochrome. Where's Johnny?"

"I don't know. He was here a moment ago," Dad said, looking here and there.

Back to the scene of the smashed thumb, Mom and I left the groceries on the ground and hurried into the house. I knew what was coming - Mercurochrome. More pain and more screaming.

The swelling and the throbbing gradually subsided over the next few days, but the greatest relief of all was that they never mentioned the whuppin' again.

Watching Radio

Mom began working as a secretary at the county court house, and Dad had steady work at Gerlach Brothers. We were moving up to lower middle-class and could afford a few luxuries.

Our first luxury was a used Zenith floor-model tube radio. A big one, the size of a chest of drawers. It had to be that huge to accommodate all the vacuum tubes, and large speakers, and the internal drum wrapped with loops of wires which was actually an adjustable antenna for receiving distant stations. This was an elaborate piece of furniture.

This marvelous box provided our nightly entertainment during the years we lived in the house by the tracks. After supper, Dad would fiddle with the dial until he located one of the two stations we could receive, and we were ready for some of our favorite programs. We knew the weekly schedule by heart.

Mom and Dad sat on the couch, while my dog, Butch, and I situated ourselves on the floor with some of my tiny, green-plastic army soldiers, tanks, and jeeps. Sitting in the living room for an hour or more, we actually "watched radio" as the stories unfolded before our eyes. Sometimes we would glance at each other to share a laugh or a surprise, but mostly our eyes were glued to the radio, where the action unfolded in vivid detail.

The 1930's through the early 1950's was the Golden Age of Radio. Comedies, game shows, cowboy adventures, and stories of mystery and suspense sparked our imagination like never before - or since.

As we listened, we engaged in the actions and emotions of the story. Sound effects, whether created or recorded, painted mental pictures for us - footsteps, grunts and groans, doors slamming, gun-shots, rain, thunder, fire crackling, babies crying.

The scripts were sprinkled with dialogue designed to draw us into the scene: "Sue, what are you looking at out that window?" or "There's blood on your forehead, Bill. What happened?" We weren't just listeners, we were eye-witnesses and participants.

One of our favorite mysteries, *The Shadow*, portrayed stories of *"the fight of one man against the forces of evil."* It opened with suspenseful organ music, followed by a slow, deep, gravelly voice, *"Who knows what evil lurks in the hearts of men? The Shadow knows. Haaa, haaa, haaa, ha."*
We were primed for a thrilling murder mystery. After the mystery was solved, the raspy-voiced announcer returned to inform us, *"Crime does not pay. The Shadow knows. Haaa, haaa, haaa, ha."*

In another favorite, *The Green Hornet,* a masked crusader, risked his life to bring criminals to justice, subjecting them to the sting of the Green Hornet. Appropriately, the show opened and closed with the penetrating sound of a hornet buzzing out of the radio and into our living room. Mom kept a fly-swatter handy, just in case.

When we heard the howling blizzard that introduced *Sergeant Preston of the Yukon*, we could hardly restrain ourselves from running to the closet to grab our winter coats for protection from the biting wind and swirling snow.

"Roff, roff," barked Yukon King, *"the swiftest and strongest lead dog of the North-West, breaking the trail for Sergeant Preston of the North-West Mounted Police in his relentless pursuit of lawbreakers."* It was set during the Gold Rush of the 1890's. Being East Texans who rarely saw snow, we shivered for the next 30 minutes.

Gangbusters opened with a patrol car siren and the rat-a-tat-tat of a machine gun. The announcer assured us that "*Gangbusters, presented in cooperation with police and federal law enforcement departments throughout the United States, is the only national program that brings you authentic police case histories.*" Then more wailing of the siren and rat-a-tat-tating, and we were mesmerized, ready for the adventure.

Every program had its own sponsors, and the heroes of each episode strongly recommended their products. Roy Rogers, the King of the Cowboys, often reminded me to try Post Cereals as a favor to him. Not wanting to disappoint Roy, I made sure that Mom kept the cupboard full of Post Cereals. I was one of his faithful "*buckaroos.*"

Roy's "*stories of the real West*" always ended with some great cowboy songs, like "Alabama Gal," and "Roll On Little Dogies," and even some with a spiritual theme, like "There Will Be Peace in the Valley," and "A Good Old-Fashioned Talk with the Lord." In conclusion, Roy often said, "*May the good Lord take a liking to you.*" I would be back next week, because he beckoned me by singing "Happy Trails to You, Until We Meet Again."

Inner Sanctum offered dramas of death and horror with a bit of comedy mixed in. Each episode began with creepy organ music, as a squeaky door sloooowly opened, and our host's spooky voice invited us into the inner sanctum. The door creaked shut and clicked. We were trapped for a half-hour of terror and enjoyed every minute of it.

Comedian Groucho Marx hosted the quiz show, *You Bet Your Life*. In interviewing the contestants, Groucho always surprised us with his off-the-cuff, sometimes insulting, always entertaining remarks. The questions were usually not too difficult to answer, and made us think we could easily win the $2000 grand prize.

The Lone Ranger, with his faithful Indian companion, Tonto, was *"the legend of a man who buried his identity to dedicate his life to the service of humanity and his country."* We would have voted for this masked cowboy as president if he had run. The show opened with "The William Tell Overture" music, a *"Hi-ho Silver,"* five bangs of a pistol, and the dynamic proclamation, *"A fiery horse with the speed of light, a cloud of dust, and a hearty 'Hi-ho Silver.' The Lone Ranger rides again."*

The Adventures of Red Rider began with the clippity-clop of hoof beats, the declaration, *"From out of the West comes America's famous fighting cowboy,"* and the opening bars of "Bury Me Not on the Long Prairie." It was a brief intro, but all we needed. The adventure began immediately.

Another of our favorites started abruptly with the music, *Dun-da-dun-dun...dun-da-dun-dun-DUUUUN.* The announcer informed us, *"The story you're about to hear is true. Only the names have been changed to protect the innocent."* We knew it was time for *Dragnet* - *"the documented drama of an actual crime."* But first, we had to listen to why we should be smoking *"Fatima cigarettes, best of all long cigarettes."* The Fatima market hadn't found Poke County yet, so I wasn't tempted.

Next, the announcer lured us into the drama, *"You're a detective sergeant assigned to the Robbery* (or Homicide) *Division."* Then he would describe *"an actual case from police files"* and give us our assignment. Actually, the assignment was Joe Friday's, but we took seriously each case, because we were told, *"Your job ... get 'em!"* We always *"got 'em."* The show ended with brief details of the trial, conviction, and sentence of the criminals. Very satisfying.

The $64 Question was a quiz show with the first question worth $1. The value doubled with each successive question. The seventh and final question, worth $64, was a big sum of money in the early 1950's. "That's the $64 question" became a common catchphrase for a particularly difficult question or problem.

Other shows we enjoyed were:

Superman – introduced by four voices, *"Up in the sky, look." "It's a bird." "It's a plane." "It's Superman!"*

The Life of Riley – a comedy that gave us the popular catch-phrase, "What a revoltin' development this is."

Sky King - harrowing adventures with an Arizona rancher who used his airplane, Songbird, to catch criminals and find lost hikers.

Burns and Allen and *Fibber McGee and Molly* – two husband and wife comedy teams which kept us laughing with their antics and jokes.

Probably our favorite of all time on radio, and later on television, was *Amos and Andy*, a comedy based on black characters in Harlem. The scripts were voiced on radio mostly by two white men who wrote and produced the show.

Amos, a philosophical, hardworking cabdriver, narrated the show, while George "Kingfish" Stephens was the main character. Kingfish often involved his gullible friend, Andy Brown, in a shady get-rich-quick scheme declaring that they were brothers in that great fraternity, the Mystic Knights of the Sea."

Several of our favorite shows made the transition to television, but they never quite held us spell-bound like the original radio productions. Television programs "spoon feed" their viewers. Radio shows invite you to engage in the action using your own imagination.

I miss watching Old Time Radio.

The Really Cool Hammock

In our side yard, between the house and the driveway, were two medium-sized trees, about 10 feet apart - a perfect place to hang my hammock, which I didn't yet have. I needed a hammock.

Most of my "brilliant ideas" required a lot of whimpering and cajoling to gain approval from my parents. This one, however, they readily accepted. I was surprised. Mom and Dad were also surprised - that I had come up with a "half-way reasonable idea, for once."

The next day, Dad purchased a sturdy, canvas hammock at the local sports store and installed it between the two trees. We three had fun trying it out and laughing at each other's attempts to conquer the hammock. Getting in, staying in, and getting out without tumbling to the ground required some practice. The hammock had several hilarious victories, but eventually we mastered it.

The hammock became part of my after-school routine. I loved getting a glass of lime sherbet and pouring some grape soda pop over it. What? You've never tried that? You should, it's delicious. This snack I took out to the side yard and carefully inserted myself into the hammock to swing and sip for the next half-hour. Life was good.

One of those afternoons, I had an inspiration.

"Why not spend a night in our hammock?" I asked myself.

No one else was around, so I had only my "Self" to help me plan how to present this proposal to my parents. I was totally on board with the idea, but my Self kept bringing up objections.

"What about wild animals? What about spooks and goblins and ghosts and other weird beings? Snakes can crawl up trees and into your hammock. It will be dark, you know."

Nonsense! I would be covered up, off the ground, within a mad-dash of the back door.

"Nothing to worry about," I told my Self.

I spent several afternoons planning how I would persuade Mom and Dad to let me spend a night in the hammock. Also, it took several afternoons to convince my Self that we would be OK. Abandoning my usual arsenal of argumentative weapons, I decided to use the "shocker" approach.

"Say, Mom and Dad, I think I'll spent tonight out in my hammock."

They gave each other a knowing look and replied, "Sure, why not?"

Suddenly, my Self whispered to me, "Now wait a minute here. What are they doing?"

I needed clarification. "You mean it's OK?"

"Sure," Dad said. "C'mon, I'll help you get some bedding ready. You know it might get a little cool out there tonight."

I couldn't be sure, but I thought I saw Mom and Dad wink at each other as Dad and I went upstairs to get some bedding.

After supper and our extended session of "watching radio," it was Friday night bedtime - 9:30. We all three went out to the hammock to arrange the sheet and blanket that would comfort me in the cool of the evening. PJ's were not needed. I snuggled into the hammock fully clothed - tennis shoes and all. My Self had reminded me that tennies would be handy in an emergency, like escaping from some of the afore-mentioned horrors lurking out in the dark.

Mom and Dad tucked me in, wished me a good night's sleep, and went back into the house. So, there I lay in my hammock, alone, all alone, no one else around, except for my Self who kept mumbling disturbing things about creatures that inhabit the night.

I lay there wide awake for what must have been hours. Finally, I dozed, but just for a minute. A cricket chirped. I bolted awake. A frog croaked, the wind rustled the leaves, and I thought I heard a snake slithering in my direction.

The moon cast creepy shadows around me, in shifting forms of the monsters my Self had warned about. I trembled so violently, there was danger of capsizing the hammock and plunging to certain death from what waited below, baring their teeth and licking their chops.

I panicked and sprung from the hammock. The back door was some 25 feet away, but it only took me four giant bounds to get there. Fortunately, in those days, no one locked their doors, otherwise I would have ripped ours off the hinges.

Safely inside, I noticed that Mom and Dad were still in the living room. Strange. What were they doing up, in the middle of the night?

"So, you decided to sleep in the house tonight? What's the matter? Wasn't the hammock comfortable?" Mom asked, with a twinkle in her eye.

Must have been because I startled her. Her eyes don't usually twinkle like that in the wee hours of the morning.

"Yeah, the hammock wasn't all that comfortable," I lied, thankful for the out, because I didn't have time to make up an excuse between the hammock and the house.

"Well, let's all get to bed," Dad said.

I agreed whole heartedly. I shut and locked the back door to make sure none of the monsters wanted to join us inside. Going upstairs I looked back at the clock in the kitchen. It said 10:00. How could that be?

"Hmmmm, musta stopped," I said to my Self. "Let's remind them to rewind the clock in the morning." Settled securely in the safety of my inside-the-house bed, I kept waking up, thinking I heard muffled giggling and whispering in the next room. Or, did I just dream it?

The next day, I was somewhat disturbed. I really hated to disappoint Mom and Dad, since they fully expected me to spend the whole night out there in my hammock. At least, I think they did.

"Sure they did," my Self said, mockingly. One's Self can be so irritating sometimes.

The Snake that Almost Killed Me

Snakes don't have to be poisonous to almost kill you. They don't even have to bite you. I have proven this truth many times from my personal encounters with the slimy creatures. Here's one example.

On one of our visits to see Uncle Roscoe and Aunt Beth Carlisle in Farmersville, Texas, I was helping Aunt Beth clean the chicken coop and gather the eggs. She raised a dozen or so chickens for their eggs and sometimes their meat. Yummy.

While the chickens busily pecked around the yard, I went into the coop to gather the eggs from their nests. I saw in one nest a neat-looking length of rope and asked Aunt Beth if I could have it.

"Hey, Aunt Beth," I yelled to her out in the yard. "Can I have this piece of rope?"

"Sure," she yelled back.

I picked up the rope. Now, as you read this, push "pause" to envision the scene. Boy is holding rope. Out in the chicken yard, Aunt suddenly freezes in wide-eyed, jaw-dropping horror, as she instantly analyzes the situation:

There is no rope in the chicken coop.
Snakes like chicken eggs.
Snakes crawl up into chicken nests.
Johnny is holding a snake.

"Don't pick up that rope. It's a snake!" she shouted.

Now, as you read, you will need to push "slow motion" to visualize what happened next, because viewing in "real time" would be too blurry. The speed of sound is about 761 miles per hour. The information, *it's a snake,* reached my brain in a millisecond, and that snake broke the sound barrier, as I hurled him vehemently against the wall of the hen house.

Now you can return to normal speed. In a few seconds the snake regained consciousness, glared at me somewhat cross-eyed, and managed a wobbly slither under the wall back to the woods.

Arriving safely at the den, his report to the wife and kids might have gone something like this:
Wife: "Honey, what happened to you? You're missing a fang, and your scales are all catawampus."
Snakelets: "Daddy, you look like cousin Hognose with your smushed face."
Snake: "It was horrible. I had just coiled up there at my usual place in the egg restaurant, getting ready for lunch, when this human hand rudely grabbed hold of me, paused a millisecond, and flung me against the wall. I think I reached Mach 1, but a blood-curdling scream drowned out the sonic boom.
Back at the chicken coop, the scene was a bit different.
Aunt: "Johnny, are you alright? Can you close your eyelids a little? You look creepy."
Johnny (with mouth agape):
Aunt: "Can you stop panting so wildly and say something?"
Johnny:
Aunt: Come on, let's go in the house and get a drink. You might want to leave your hands there clutching your chest to keep your heart in. It sounds like a bass drum."
Walking through the yard, I noticed the chickens were flapping and clucking around wildly. A scattering of feathers wafted down to the ground like huge snowflakes. Maybe it was the scream, or maybe the boom, but the chickens were definitely in a dither.
I'm not sure if seven-year-old boys can have heart attacks from fright, but I came mighty close to performing one. The perp was probably just a harmless rat snake - some four feet long. I didn't take time to go look it up in the *Encyclopedia Britannica* before reacting.
You see what I mean, that snakes don't have to bite you to almost kill you?

WHAT WERE THINGS LIKE IN THE 1950s?

Let's take a break from the stories and examine the 50s era. Some have referred to the Fabulous 50s as the Golden Era, which is now lost. Although we experienced the Cold War, racial tension, and fear of communism, we also enjoyed an increase in affluence. We became a unified, middle-class nation under a stable government led by president Dwight Eisenhower. In our carefree spirit, we were blissfully unaware of the chaos and turmoil that loomed ahead in the 60s.

What things cost in 1955

Below are some average $ signs for the year 1955 - my thirteenth year of life. Again, you should put "plus or minus" in front of each of these, meaning "somewhere around."

New house – $9,100
Rent – $180/month
New car – $1,700
Gas – 23¢ a gallon
Minimum wage – 75¢ an hour
Average annual income – $3,400
Member of US Congress salary – $22,500
Postage stamp – 3¢ (same as 1945)
One year tuition at Harvard – $1000
Computer – IBM 650 - $3200 rent per month, weighs one ton, measures 5-feet by 3-feet by 6-feet

(Until 1955, the word "computer" referred to people who performed computations, not to a machine. By the end of the 50s, we spoke of "digital computers," while a "calculator" was the clunky thing on your desk.

The 50s ushered in:
McDonalds Drive-in movies
The barcode Credit cards
3D movies Mr. Potato Head
Pace maker Hula Hoop
Barbie Doll Roll-on deodorant
Diet soft drink Teflon
Polio vaccine Hydrogen bomb
TV dinners Color TV
Bubble wrap

Slang of the 50s

As pre-baby-boomers, we teenagers still held to the traditional values of hard work, respect, loyalty, and thriftiness, however we were coming of age. We created a vernacular that expressed our desire for independence and liberation. Most of these have gone the way of the Edsel:

Cruisin' for a bruisin' = looking for trouble
Daddy-O/Cool cat = a cool dude
Burn rubber = accelerate a car rapidly
Got it made in the shade = in a comfortable position
Go ape = get really mad
Church key = can opener
Wet rag/party pooper = nerd, a boring person, no fun
Catch a flick = go to a movie
A square = a conformist, not "hip"
Make like a tree and leave = go away
Beatnik = a youth into music, drugs, etc
Birddog = one who steals a girl friend
Horn = telephone
Cheaters = eye glasses
Going steady = boyfriend and girlfriend
Nifty = great, cool
A bash = a party
Classy chassis = great body (for girls)
Have a cow = freak out
Rattle your cage = make you angry/annoyed

To split = to leave
Threads, duds = clothes
Bread = money
To dig = to understand, approve
Hep = cool, with it, in style

Some interesting history of the 50s

- The Korean War, from 1950-53, began as a civil war, but escalated to a war between Western powers against Communist China and the Soviet Union.
- In 1954, runner, Roger Bannister, broke the 4-minute mile.
- In 1955, Rosa Parks' refusal to vacate her seat aboard a Montegomery, Alabama bus sparked the civil rights movement of the 60s.
- The Interstate Highway System began in 1956.
- The Space Race began in 1957 with the Soviet Union's launch of Sputnik 1.
- Alaska and Hawaii became the 49th and 50th states in 1959.

American culture in the 50s

Rebelliousness began to raise its ugly head in the 50s and blossomed in the 60s. In the 50s, we teens conformed to the popular hairstyles, allowing the rebellion to manifest itself. Elvis Presley and Sal Mineo influenced us with the pompadour – longer hair, greased up on top and slicked down on the sides. The trendies earned the fitting nickname "greasers." Marlon Brando and James Dean lured us to add long sideburns.

The flattop spoke less of rebellion and more of conforming. In Poke County many of us preferred this short haircut with the top appearing as a flat deck, either level or sloping downward. Butch Wax stiffened the hair to make it stand up.

Unfortunately for me, my head-shape necessitated a bald spot in the middle to accommodate the "flat" look. Very embarrassing, but necessary - so I thought. But that was OK. Two of my sports idols had flattops - Johnny Unitas and Roger Maris.

For the duck tail, the hair is longer, combed back around the sides, and parted centrally down the back of the head. It resembled the rear end of a duck.

This could only be accomplished with "ruly" hair - mine was unruly. Mom explained that I had "cow licks" all over my head, because my hair grew in many different directions. I looked like a ragamuffin in most of my elementary school pictures.

The duck tail needed grease to keep it in place. Brylcreem enticed guys to buy tubes of the stuff with their jingle, "Brylcreem, a little dab'll do ya. Brylcreem, the gals will pursue ya." I tried it. Didn't work.

We had heard of the Mohawk, or Mohican, and had even seen pictures, but none of us dared try it. Both sides of the head are shaved, leaving a strip of longer hair in the center. The strip could be narrow or wide.

Once, a friend, Runnie DeFaster, vowed to get a Mohawk. Several of us high schoolers accompanied him during lunch-break to the barber shop to make sure he followed through.

The barber hesitated, but said, "OK, if you insist," and produced a fantastic Mohawk.

Back at school, the teachers were upset, but the rest of us cheered. We nicknamed him "Runnie the Brave." I suspect his parents were also upset. The next day, his Mohawk became a very short burr haircut. His nickname changed to "Runnie the Shaved."

I asked my wife about the girls' hairstyles. She said ponytails and pageboys. I had to look up pageboy. The hair reaches the shoulder and is rolled under the ends. Often there are bangs in the front.

I do remember Lucille Ball's poodle cut, Sophia Loren's bouffant, and Audrey Hepburn's pixie. In general, housewives wore short hair, youth wore medium, and Hollywood pin ups wore long hair. I kept pictures of the latter hidden safely in a dresser drawer.

Dance and music of the 50s

Terminology was just as varied as the dancing. We had the jitterbug, swing, rock'n'roll, and boogie-woogie. The word "bop" was new then, so almost everything was called The Bop.

Music marketing began to target youth. Elvis Presley enthralled us and scandalized our parents with his suggestive lyrics and dance moves. Chuck Berry, Fats Domino, and Buddy Holly added to the emergence of the new sound sweeping the nation. It helped inspire the rockabilly music of Jerry Lee Lewis and Johnny Cash.

Movies of the 50s

Popular movie stars included Tony Curtis, Marlon Brando, Gary Cooper, Jerry Lewis, Frank Sinatra, Burt Lancaster, Doris Day, Debbie Reynolds, Grace Kelly, Elizabeth Taylor, and my favorites – Elvis Presley and Marilyn Monroe.

I practiced Elvis's songs, pelvis-swinging, and guitar playing, in front of my bedroom mirror - alone, with no audience. Actually, you are the first to hear about this.

Then there was Marilyn. We guys liked her... well, we were guys, you know.

Maybe you've seen some of our favorite movies: *Gunfight at the O.K. Corral, High Noon, Around the World in 80 Days, The Ten Commandments, South Pacific, From Here to Eternity,* and *Cat on a Hot Tin Roof.*

Concerning that last one, let it be known that I only saw the first portion. The Fain didn't offer us those juicy kinds of movies, so we had to go to Houston to view it. I got convicted and left the theater in embarrassment.

We also loved the scary movies. *Invasion of the Body Snatchers* told of people falling asleep and being replaced with identical-looking imposters, which emerged from giant seed pods. The replacements were devoid of humanity. Everyone struggled to stay awake, and we in the audience had no trouble doing so. The movie ends with the warning, "They're here! You're next." A good night's sleep was a long time coming, after that movie.

In *The Thing*, a UFO crashes at the North Pole, and a frozen monster-like body is rescued. When the creature is accidentally thawed, it attacks everyone, feasting on their blood, but is finally electrocuted and reduced to a pile of dust. Before the large printed words, "The End," appeared on screen, a calculated voice instructed us, "Tell the world. Tell this to everybody. Watch the skies everywhere. Keep looking. Keep watching the skies". We walked out of the theater with heads turned to the sky, and kept them up for several days.

Horse and Buggy Days of the 40s and 50s
So, our grandkids ask us what else we did in the "dinosaur days?"
Well......
We chewed Black Jack gum and small Coke-shaped wax
    bottles with colored sugar-water.
We ate candy cigarettes.
We watched news reels before the picture show.
We donned card-frame eyeglasses with red and blue filters to
    read 3-D comic books and watch 3-D movies.
We ate at diners with table-side jukeboxes.
Girls wore poodle skirts, bobby sox, and saddle shoes.
Guys rolled up the cuff of their jeans and wore tennies.
We played stick ball or rag ball.
We rode in cars without seat belts.
We played board games like Scrabble, Yahtzee and Carroms.
We joined the "Peanut Gallery" to interact with Howdy
    Doody and Buffalo Bob

We joined the Mickey Mouse Club.
Boys wore a Davy Crockett coonskin cap.
We watched movies at drive-in movies.
We hunted for and chopped down live Christmas trees in the open woods and brought them home to decorate.
We played jacks, marbles, red rover red rover, hopscotch, mother may I, freeze tag, and kick the can

According to our grandchildren, we used weird idioms and expressions.

To express surprise, we said:
    Well, I'll be a monkey's uncle!   Heavens to Betsy!
    Jumping Jehoshaphat!   Holy Moley!

If things were going our way, we said:
    Hunky Dory.   Fine as frog hair.
    Right as rain.   Living the life of Riley.
    In like Flynn.

If not going our way, we said:
    This is a fine kettle of fish.
    Well, fiddlesticks.
    Aw, shucks.

When greeting or departing we said:
    I'll see you in the funny papers.   See ya later, alligator.
    Not if I see you first.   After while, crocodile.
    Don't take any wooden nickels.

    In June 1954, *Life* magazine published an article about teenagers of the 50s entitled "The Luckiest Generation." I agree. The 1950's were a great decade to be a teenager. I loved it.

    Want to learn more about the 50s?
Just watch some TV episodes of: Or, maybe the movies:
    Happy Days,   *The West Side Story,*
    Laverne and Shirley,   *Back to the Future,*
    Father Knows Best,   *Grease.*
    Leave It to Beaver.

THE HOUSE ON CALHOUN
1952-1960
5th Grade through High School

Moving to Calhoun Street

By the summer of 1952, I had survived four years of servitude in The Alamo. Both of my parents were working and had saved enough money to buy our own house. We could now be called lower middle-class. The house, at 917 W. Calhoun Street, sat on a half-acre of land, near the west end of Livingston.

I didn't find the street name as entertaining as did my friends. One of our favorite radio programs, *Amos and Andy*, had a humorous character named Calhoun, a self-educated, sometimes shady lawyer. My friends thought it was funny that I'd moved to a street with that same name.

But that's OK. We had a great house, and I had a huge back yard and a waiting-to-be-explored forest across that front street named Calhoun. I was happy.

Our new mansion was a three-bedroom wood-frame, built on pier and beam. My dog, Butch, and I enjoyed crawling in the dry sand under the house, pretending to explore a cave.

A solid interior wall from front to back divided the house neatly into two sections. From the front door to the back door was a straight shot, through the living room, then the dining room, then the kitchen.

The other half of the house had three bedrooms and a bathroom, all connected by a small hallway. So, who would have which bedroom?

In the house by the tracks, Dad's snoring was not a problem. No snoring could out-volume the trains that roared within 100 feet of that residence. But our new house presented a dilemma - no loud train to drown out the snoring.

So, Mom, being a very light sleeper, took the large front bedroom, Dad, the tiny back bedroom, and I got the medium-sized middle bedroom.

I could hardly believe my good fortune. I had a full-size bed with bookshelf headboard, a six-drawer chest-o-drawers with large mirror, and a two-drawer student desk. My princely quarters.

Dad was an amateur, self-taught carpenter. He installed a large attic fan in the ceiling of the hallway, which sucked air to provide a breeze through open windows. The air exited to the outside through louvers in the back wall of the attic. This made summers bearable until we finally got a window cooler - the precursor to air-conditioning.

Before flipping the "on" switch for the attic fan, you just had to be certain to open the hall doors, otherwise, the fan's motor would burn out and maybe even burn up the house.

Another hazard was forgetting to open the windows. My parents said this would cause a strong vacuum to build, sucking up furniture, pets, and people into the fan's blades. Not a pretty sight to imagine. Probably that's the reason they often reminded me of these consequences.

"Johnny, don't you dare forget to open the hall doors and a few windows if you turn on the attic fan," they often admonished. "You don't want to burn up the house, or get sucked up into those blades, along with Butch and the furniture."

Parents have devious ways of controlling their children's behavior. Looking back, I wonder why I never gave it a try just to see how much furniture the fan could slurp up into its hungry blades.

For heat, we had a small, gas heater with ceramic grates, in the living room. It fought valiantly to keep the temperature bearable in all six rooms during the chilly winters. We slept under thick quilts and fluffy comforters.

Dad also built a combination two-car garage and storage shed at the end of the driveway, and a five-by-eight-foot storage room on half of the back porch. He used those and other projects to teach me some valuable carpentry skills at an early age. I could hammer a nail, saw a board, twist a brace and bit, and wield a flat-head screwdriver better than any of my friends. Power tools and Phillips-head screws were a thing of the future.

Settling into the house on Calhoun Street was easy. It became my home for 13 years, until Diana and I married in 1965. Oh, the memories I cherish, and the stories I could tell!

My Back Yard

None of my friends had a back yard like mine. Most of them lived in larger houses with smaller yards. I felt sorry for them. Our small house sat on two full lots on the west edge of town, bordered front and back by two dirt roads.

The front lot contained, from front street to clothesline, a small front yard, the house and garage, a small back yard, a huge pine tree, five medium-sized oak trees, and the clothesline - stretched between two oaks. The back lot was completely empty - no fences in those days. In fact, we seldom ever locked our houses.

My back yard became a sports arena where I could play alone, with friends, with smaller neighborhood kids, or even with my parents. Activities included football, baseball, louver-ball, whiffle ball, basketball, horseshoes, washers, BB gun and bow-and-arrow ranges, Hide and Seek, Annie Over, and crawdad fishing. Some of these may require explanation.

We called the yard between the house and clothesline "the back yard," and the vacant lot "the back lot." These together seemed, in my young mind, to be as big as a football field, and twice that size when I mowed it with our push mower.

Football was the most popular sport, played by all participants, except Mom, and played on both fields.

"But you said you played alone sometimes. How do you play football alone?" you ask.

I had several ways. Using my kicking tee - a small, scooped up mound of dirt - I practiced kicking field goals over the garage into the neighbor's yard. I practiced passing by zipping tight spirals to an imaginary receiver running beside the garage wall. Observers might have described my tosses as fluttering wobbles.

I had plenty of room for punting practice, but after a few times chasing the ball the length of the back lot, I opted to work on the skill of punting it straight up in the air as high as possible and catching it.

This was fun, until the time I ran into the clothesline pole tooth-first as a 12-year-old. Looking up, with mouth wide open, I chased an errant punt and cracked a top front tooth against the pole. It hurt. Stunned, I staggered to the bathroom mirror to see if I was permanently deformed. A neat crack line appeared across the tooth, but it was still intact. That tooth is still in my mouth, although it has browned slightly through the decades.

Having neither the size nor the inclination to be a football lineman, I worked on my receiving skills. Enter Dad, my quarterback. Many an afternoon I waited, with football in hand, for him to come home from work. After a quick cup of coffee, he threw me pass after pass, until I wore him out. He was quite an athlete in his day, in fact, a gifted receiver in high school and college.

Zig zagging and cutting around the back yard, I developed a skill for snagging passes at full speed, with my hands, not my chest. Later on, in college and seminary, I made the all-star team in flag football with that skill.

Next, you may ask, "How do you play baseball alone?"

I had several ways. Aspiring to be an outstanding infielder, I threw a tennis ball against the garage countless times, learning to gage the bouncing rebound and field it smoothly.

For fly balls, I threw the tennis ball against the attic louvers above the back porch. If thrown hard enough, the ball took unpredictable rebounds off the louvers, serving up challenging fly balls. For batting, I had my batting range, but that's another story - later.

Whiffle ball, a variation of baseball, was a two-boy sport. The ball is plastic with holes to make it "whiffle" with curves and dips, and the bat is hollow plastic. Our multipurpose garage served as the backstop behind home plate. A pitcher and a batter were all you needed.

We marked off boundaries in the back yard using trees, side of the house, boxes, large pine cones - whatever was available. These borders indicated the required distance a batted whiffle ball must travel in the air to be a single, double, triple, or homerun. Homeruns had to travel the width of the yard, avoiding tree limbs, and land over the ditch that separated our yard with the neighbors'. Homers were rare.

The batter never ran, just hit, because bases weren't used. A grounder in front of the singles line meant an out. Strike outs and caught flies were also outs.

Both players announced the action of the game to the imaginary fans in attendance. Base runners, balls and strikes, and score were announced with each pitch, to help us keep track.

Sometimes the umpires' calls were hotly contested. The fans loved it and joined in the rhubarb. Often, the announcers got carried away with their commentary. We knew how to pretend and make our own entertainment.

For basketball, Dad set up a deluxe goal in the back lot. Let me describe "deluxe." He found the discarded portion of a tele-phone pole and bolted a backboard to it. The backboard was a four-foot, wheel-shaped, wooden side of a huge cable spool - ugly, but cheap and usable.

He found a metal basketball rim at the dump and installed it. With posthole diggers he dug a three-foot hole for the pole and erected the unsightly assembly. It wasn't pretty. The rim was about three inches higher than regulation, and the heavy wooden backboard caused the apparatus to waggle slightly with every shot.

But I had my personal basketball goal on my personal court. I was proud of it. Later, Dad splurged and bought a 15-cent net and attached it to the rim.

Mine was the only basketball court my friends and I had. They were jealous. I developed a fairly decent set-shot on that court and had an advantage when I shot at regulation goals. They were four inches shorter.

Mom played only one sport with us - basketball. A star player in high school, she won All County honors as a senior.

The three major sports were accommodated. But that's not all. Washers and horseshoes were played. We began with washers.

I just now checked online and discovered you can buy a complete set of Official Washers for $40-70. Ours set cost $40-70 less than that.

Dad found a set of four two-and-one-half inch metal washers in his tool box, and dug two holes in the ground, about four inches in diameter, set about 15 feet apart. Not having the official set of rules that comes with the modern, expensive game, he used "about" as his standard of measurement.

Then Dad taught me how to play. You stand at one hole and throw the washers into the other hole. In-the-hole counts three points, leaning-partly-over-the-hole counts two, and closest-to-the-hole, one point. Sounded easy.

"OK, Johnny, you take two washers and I take two. I'll go first," he said, and sailed his first washer into the hole. His second one slid smoothly up close to the hole.

"See, that's not difficult. Now you give it a try."

My hands are still small today, but my eight-year-old hands were tiny. Those washers felt big and heavy. Tentatively, I gave the first washer an underhand toss in the general direction of the hole, which now seemed more like 30 feet away. Like a wounded bird, it flailed its way in an arch, landing with a thud, bouncing and rolling away from the hole.

Dad laughed. I didn't. *How did he make that washer sail so flatly, like a flying saucer?*

"You don't grab it like a baseball and heave it end over end," he explained. "Here let me show you. Rest the washer on your middle finger, with forefinger wrapped around the front, and thumb on top. Let it spin out of your hand."

I tried it. It worked! Beginning with that second toss I developed into a fairly competitive washer player. I loved having friends over and teaching them how to toss a washer properly. And best of all, I could usually beat them.

Not long after that, I heard about horseshoes and began my campaign to own a set.

"You don't want to deprive some poor horse of his shoes, do you?" Dad teased.

Not knowing what a set of "pitching horseshoes" looked like, I thought he was serious. The next Christmas a brand new, store-bought set of horseshoes appeared under the tree. It was like my best Christmas ever.

Dad and I pounded-in the metal stakes for my new horse shoe pit in a sandy area of the back yard. He also had experience pitching horseshoes, so began my lessons, demonstrating a couple of tosses.

He used the flat-toss style. The horseshoe flies flat in the air, making a 360-degree turn, landing with open-end facing the stake, and neatly wrapping around it. Dad's two tosses landed close to the stake, and one was a "ringer" - wrapped around the pole. Looked easy.

"Like this, huh, Dad?" I gave it a toss with all my might. *Hmmm...not as easy as it looks,* I thought to myself. Mom, watching off to the side, gasped as she dodged the wayward horseshoe. Dad enjoyed a good laugh.

Mom moved a safer distance away, and I tried my second throw. No improvement. We retrieved our horseshoes and prepared to take aim at the other stake. I decided that Dad's throwing style wasn't for me.

I grabbed the horseshoe in the middle and held it out in front of me, parallel to the ground. Keeping it flat, I swung it behind me, then forward, like a softball pitcher, and heaved it in an arch straight toward the stake. En route, the horseshoe made several backward flips and landed fairly close to the stake. We all cheered.

I had discovered a horseshoe pitching technique that would win me honors and acclaim as a champion horseshoe tosser in the years to follow. I became practically unbeatable. But that deserves another story with explanation - in my next book. Well, OK, if you insist, I'll tell it now.

After weeks of practice, I could make about 40% ringers and sometimes double ringers. That summer, as an eight-year-old, I went to my first Royal Ambassador camp with some other Central Baptist Church boys at Pineywoods Baptist Encampment, 40 miles northwest of Livingston.

My friend, Garner Brock, and I were the smallest boys at camp. He also loved horseshoes, so we signed up for the tournament. Miraculously, we won the tourney, even against the high schoolers. In one of the matches, I covered a double ringer. That's almost unheard of.

At awards night, we walked down the aisle to receive our first-place ribbons, and someone commented aloud, "They don't even look big enough to pick up the horseshoes." That was our moment of glory.

BB gun and bow-and-arrow ranges also found a home in my large back lot - probably because no other parents were inclined to host such events in their small yards.

Mom strongly suggested, "Don't you dare shoot that BB gun or that bow and arrow in the direction of the house! Put your targets far away out there in the back lot."

I had to demonstrate to her that neither my BB gun nor my homemade bow had the power to send their projectiles from the end of the back lot to our house. Finally, she allowed us to shoot in the direction of the house, convinced it was in no danger. The targets weren't in much danger either. In our preteen years, none of us were master marksmen or bowmen.

Our house and yards were perfect for Hide and Seek and Annie Over. The door-less garage, the huge trees, the ditch in the back, and the crawl space under the house made for good Hiding and Seeking. With open space all around, the house was ideal for Annie Over.

Besides sports, my back yard taught me gardening and treehouse building. Some of my friends at school lived on a farm,
and wore cool jackets to identify them as Future Farmers of America. I had no idea how to farm.

"Hey, Mom and Dad, how do you farm?" I asked one day.

Both of them had some experience. In fact, they almost bought a farm outside Livingston instead of our house on Calhoun. I might have been in FFA, raised farm animals, and tended a vegetable garden. That would have been cool, but didn't happen.

"Shucks, it's easy. You just throw some seeds out on the ground and they grow," Dad explained. "Wanna try it?"

Mom intervened, "No! It takes more than that."

She liked radishes and knew they were easy to grow, so the next day she brought home a package of radish seeds. Together we hoed a small garden plot in the back lot under the shade of an oak.

My garden was roughly the dimensions of a card table - not too ambitious an undertaking. Mom showed me how to dig half-inch holes a couple of inches apart. We inserted a seed in each hole, covered it with dirt, and watered the new garden.

I ran outside the next morning to see if any radishes had appeared. They hadn't.

Dad suggested, "Maybe the garden goblin gobbled 'em." That's not easy to say while laughing. Mom assured me I could see some sprouts in a few days.

She proved right. After four days some green growth magically peeked out of the soil. It was so exciting. I wanted to harvest the radishes immediately, but Mom said it would take four weeks for them to mature. A month is a long time for a new farmer to wait.

One day Mom announced, "I think you can pull up some radishes today, Johnny."

I protested, "But Mom, there are no radishes showing yet."

She taught me how to carefully hold the bushy top and slowly lift the radish. It was a miracle. A healthy red radish, about the size of a ping pong ball, emerged from under the half inch of soil. I had become a farmer.

Every boy needs a treehouse to play in and brag about. One afternoon, we were resting from a session of football catching practice, and I ventured, "Hey, Dad, how about we build a treehouse in the back yard."

I wasn't sure what to expect. Turns out, he liked the idea as much as I did. He enjoyed building things.

The back corner of the back yard had a spot just begging for a treehouse. Three oak trees formed a triangle about eight feet apart - perfect location.

Dad had some lumber left over from building the garage and back porch closet. He also found some rather rugged looking lumber and rusty nails at the dump. This was going to be a low-budget treehouse, and it would take several weeks to construct.

First, we nailed three two-by-fours to connect the three trees. This would be the floor foundation, about seven feet off the ground. With more two-by-fours we built a ladder from the ground to where the door would be. We nailed some reasonably flat, smooth boards to form the floor. This involved several bent nails and smashed thumbs, and loud screams, but finally I learned how to hit the nail on the head every time.

Next, the protruding floor boards needed to be sawed off to be flush with the foundation. This was work for the "grunt" - me. Dad taught me how to use a handsaw. That's a skill learned with a lot of sweat and nicked fingers. Not that easy for a nine-year-old grunt, but I wanted that treehouse, so I persevered.

The completed floor became the platform from which we finished the sides and the roof with more boards of varying quality. We also built a door and a window.

In the construction process, some of my friends came to help. I had advanced from grunt to apprentice, adeptly wielding hammer and saw. My friends were still at the grunt level. They bent nails and got frustrated at the handsaw. Dad, the amateur carpenter, had passed on to me some valuable skills which proved very useful the rest of my life.

That treehouse became my combination Fortress/Kingdom/Hideaway. Friends and I defended it from invading armies. We ate snacks and read comic books there. Once my fifth-grade class held a class party in my back yard, and everyone was sooo impressed with my treehouse. I even found solitude there to contemplate life's bewilderments - *What's the meaning of life?* and *Why don't girls like me?*

Over the years, the three oaks grew at different rates. The treehouse morphed into a carnival-like fun house, with slanting floor, catawampus walls, and sinking roof. It became unsafe for occupancy and needed to be decommissioned. That was a sad day for both Dad and me. Mom, though, was glad to get rid of what had become that "ghastly monstrosity."

And finally - crawdads. For you who are not fortunate enough to have been raised in a place like Poke County, let me explain crawdad fishing. Depending on where the little creatures reside, they may be called crayfish, crawfish, mudbugs, or mountain lobsters. We called them crawdads. These fresh water crustaceans come in many varieties, resemble miniature lobsters, and have pinchers.

The edible kind are delicious, but I only caught them for the fun of it - catch and release. Along the drainage ditch bordering our back lot, the crawdads dug their little holes, leaving a neat mound of mud above and around the hole. If you tie a tiny piece of bacon on a string and lower it into the hole, the crawdad will grab it with his pincher, and you can pull him up out of his hole.

OK, it's not really all that easy. It takes patience, a slow steady pull, and multiple tries, because Mr. Crawdad will usually let go just as you get him to the surface. After several attempts you may need to go try another crawdad hole which, hopefully, will house a less cagey crawdad.

If you succeed in catching one, you have to hold it just right to avoid the pinchers. Then you can put it down and watch it scamper back into its hole, or better yet, take it to school the next day to scare the girls with. As I said before, we learned to make our own entertainment.

My back yard and I were made for each other at just the right time in my life. Recently, I revisited Livingston and drove the front and back streets bordering our former house on Calhoun.

Things have changed. The house has expanded and changed colors. The once inviting, "y'all come sit a spell," front porch is closed in. Dad's custom-made garage is replaced by a larger one with a door.

A house now sits on the back lot, and fences have appeared. Both roads are paved, and the drainage ditch is now a concrete culvert - bye-bye crawdads. In fact, bye-bye everything that once provided a growing boy the perfect playground for eight years.

Well, at least the fun-filled memories are still there. I'll just try to forget the modernization that now defaces my house and back yard on Calhoun, and stick with the glorious memories.

The Turkey Give-Away

The turkey almost got away. At one point I hoped he would. The scene was the parking lot across the street from Livingston's only movie theater, The Fain. During the month of November, movie patrons saved their ticket stubs in hope of winning one of four turkeys to be given away on Saturday before Thanksgiving.

The crowd that late afternoon was mostly kids who had just enjoyed another cowboy picture show. We probably saw a Roy Rogers or Gene Autry movie, but it could have been Hopalong Cassidy or Lash LaRue or "Whip" Wilson. Didn't make us much difference - we worshipped them all.

Mack, Willard, and I were there for the "Turkey Give-Away," fantasizing we would win one for our family. While waiting for the proceedings, we crammed our ticket stubs in our blue jean pockets and conducted an impromptu dirt clod fight across the street.

Finally, the announcement was made, and we rushed to join the hopeful throng, which in Livingston meant maybe three dozen people. Wiping the sweat from our brows and arms, we held our crumpled ticket stubs in our dirty little hands. The fantasy was about to be real - just like the cowboy movie was real.

Trembling with anticipation, we listened to three ticket stub numbers called out - none of which matched ours. One number remained. Could it be...?

What followed is still a little sketchy in my memory. The final number was announced and a lot of shouting and jumping around ensued - particularly by my friends and me. My stub number had been called!

In the midst of the hysteria maybe I fainted, maybe Mack slapped me on the back too hard - can't remember. Anyway, Mack hoisted me on his shoulders and ushered me in a cloud of dust to the front of the crowd where three other happy winners awaited the awarding of their turkeys.

The Master of Ceremonies, Mr. Stumpmaker, was always running for some public office and never succeeding. He took the opportunity to campaign until the impatient crowd clamored for the turkeys to be distributed. Mack and Willard had already lost interest and wandered off somewhere - probably back home, because the daylight was also gradually leaving us.

Mr. Stumpmaker merciful finished his ramblings, and the turkeys were brought forward squawking and flapping their wings. They were scary looking. Maybe they had a foreboding of their imminent fate. I, on the other hand, had no such premonition of the mayhem that loomed in my immediate future. I had won a turkey! I was ecstatic!

The first three lucky winners were beefy adult men who accepted their turkeys for their family and manhandled them to their pickups. I was last. Mr. Stumpmaker extended my turkey to my awaiting arms. It was as big as me, maybe bigger. In turkey years he was an overgrown teenager with a bad attitude.

We eyed one another. The berserk foul with menacing claws and beak, and the skinny nine-year-old boy trembling in excitement - and terror. My fantasy had not anticipated this scenario.

I stood there, frozen in horror, so Mr. Stumpmaker shoved the turkey into my chest and released it. The turkey wanted loose, but I was afraid he would use his freedom to rip me apart. I held on for dear life. Wide-eyed spectators observed the fiasco, discussing the possible outcomes. Lots of screeching and thrashing around - by both boy and bird.

Now I needed to figure out how to get my prize home - about a mile away. I had ridden my bike to the theater. Should I tie the turkey on the bike? Front or back? Maybe I should wring its neck and give both of us the relief we desperately wanted.

I managed to get half way across the street, maneuvering toward my bike parked at the side of the theater. At that moment, my parents were returning from a leisurely Saturday afternoon drive in my dad's pickup. They were a block away from the theater and glanced down the street, curious at the commotion in the middle of the road. Slowing down they looked closer at the spectacle.

Mom, not recognizing me, asked, *"What's that turkey doing?"*

Dad did recognize me and replied, *"Not sure, but he's got an arm load of screeching feathers and wings. We better go help him."*

Parents have a way of showing up when you least expect them. Usually it's unwelcomed, but this time I was overjoyed. I had been rescued!

Bicycle, boy, and protesting turkey were deposited in the back of Dad's pickup, and we headed home. The turkey and I got better acquainted on the trip. He calmed down and changed his survival strategy from hysterical thrashing to woeful, pleading stares into my eyes. I felt pity, and tried to console him by explaining that he was our guest - we were taking him home for Thanksgiving dinner.

Facing a Timber Rattler

For those not familiar with the numerous poisonous snakes of East Texas, let me acquaint you with the timber rattlesnake. This written introduction will be considerably less traumatic for you than an actual encounter. The timber rattler is one of North America's most dangerous snakes. It has long fangs, impressive size, and produces a high venom yield. In fact, it's the second largest venomous snake in Texas and the third largest in the United States. With yellow eyes and elliptical pupils, he's a nasty-looking villain.

There are two dangerous ways to meet one personally. First, you might be hiking in the woods and step over a fallen log. Don't do that! Look first. The timber rattler loves to coil there awaiting prey, like birds and small rodents. You're not prey, but he considers any intruder a threat to his well-being, and will let you know about it.

Another common way to chance upon a timber rattler is…well, I'll tell you a story. This near-death experience happened on a camping trip when I was about nine years old. A group of guys went to a friend's farm for an over-nighter. That afternoon, we organized a game of hide-and-seek in the woods.

The designated "It" instructed us, "Y'all go hide. I'll close my eyes and count to 100. First one I find is the next "it."

We scattered like a bunch of playful puppies, searching for the best hiding place. I picked out a large oak tree with low-hanging branches - ideal for climbing. I could ascend high in the oak and conceal myself in the foliage.

"Ready or not, here I come," yelled It.

Needing to scamper on up the tree, I grabbed the lowest branch, about eye level, and gazed up to plan my strategy. Looking where I had placed my hand, I prepared to swing a leg over the limb. Then I froze. Just inches away, glaring at me with a menacing scowl, was a deadly timber rattler, coiled and ready for battle.

I would like to say that with calculated calmness, I slowly backed away from the killer, expertly averting certain death. But since my stories are based on actual happenings, I will attempt to describe the next few split-seconds in vivid detail. I bolted backwards like a circus performer shot out of a cannon, shrieking the whole 20-foot flight.

The other guys abandoned their hiding places to check out the blood curdling scream. They found me sprawled on the ground, pointing at the tree, stuttering, "R-r-r-rattle s-s-s-snake!!" Meanwhile, the serpent had disappeared, lending suspicion to my claim.

Punctuating my description with gasps and shudders, I explained the harrowing encounter, "It was long as a... right there on the... coiled next to my... I coulda been... you shoulda seen... the fangs were like...."

They laughed and sneered. No snake was in sight, and they knew my reputation as a practical joker. However, in the event my account was truthful, they decided to cancel hide-and-seek, and try another activity - closer to the farm house - not in the woods.

So, I repeat, snakes don't have to bite you to almost kill you. And I will add, snakes don't have to be seen personally to make young boys fearful believers.

The Batting Range

Kids who love baseball today can have their parents pay big bucks for practice in a batting cage, and sessions with a personal hitting coach. I loved baseball, but my parents could not afford any of that, even if it were available. As a junior high kid, I wanted to improve my batting. I needed a batting cage.

Our driveway stretched some 100 feet from our garage in the back yard to the front street. Traffic was no problem on our dead-end street, because only two neighbors lived down the road. The driveway was made of dirt and small pebbles which ranged in size from B-Bs to large marbles. Dad had an extra ax handle in the storage room behind our garage, so, one afternoon, I decided to make myself a batting range - that's a batting cage without the cage.

Standing in front of my garage, I faced the front road looming 100 feet in the distance. With the ax handle in my right hand and resting on my right shoulder, I selected a small marble sized rock from the driveway and tossed it straight up in the air. The pitcher had offered a fastball over the center of the plate, and I took a whiff at it with my ax handle bat. "Whiff" meaning I missed it completely. Tried again with same result.

I struck out three times on nine pitches before I finally made connection. The fans and players from both teams cheered wildly. I took a bow and waved my cap. I had a great imagination.

By the end of a half hour I had lofted, lined, and skipped several projectiles further up the driveway. A few made it to the street - also made of dirt and pebbles. One even flew over the street, beyond the barbed wire fence, into the vacant field. Most, however, veered off into our yard or the neighbor's yard, or lodged on our tin roof.

"What are all these pebbles doing in our side yard?" Dad asked.

"Beats me," I explained.

My parents and neighbors would be coming home from work soon, so I hastily disassembled my batting range - meaning I put the ax handle back in the storage room.

In the following weeks, the batting range morphed into a full-sized Yankee Stadium. On many afternoons, the New York Yankees, my favorite team, would play another Major League team. We played a nine-inning game, and I kept the score in my head, announcing the play-by play action just like a radio announcer.

Here's how it worked. I, of course, was the lone batter, but I honestly tried my best for both teams. There were no walks. One swing and miss counted as a strike out. Most games had a lot of strikeouts.

Any baseball - which a casual observer might insist was really just a rock - that didn't reach the front street in the air was a ground out. A ball hitting the street - a single. A ball hit over the fence - a double. Triples and homers were much more difficult.

Stretched high above the fence were electric and telephone cables. If a hit ball threaded the wires, the batter got a triple, and a hit clearing all the wires was a home run. Some pretty exciting games took place at my batting range. Occasionally, I had to retrieve some baseballs from the road and the yard to replenish the balding driveway.

Early on, I informed my parents about my secret batting range and demonstrated it to them. They were mildly impressed and not at all shocked. By this time, they had learned to expect the unexpected from me, and had abandoned "shock," "horror," "disgust," and such reactions to things I did.

They simply said, *"Well, watch out for cars,"* and *"Don't break any house windows - ours or the neighbors."*

Parents have enough to worry about, so the fact that I already had several narrow misses was not necessary information to share with them. As far as I know, the two neighbors down the road never identified the UFOs zipping in front of their windshields as they casually drove by our house some afternoons.

Sometimes they came home before 5:00, and the game was still in progress. Soon they learned to zoom past our house, and the roar of the revved engine warned me to drop the ax handle, turn, and walk away nonchalantly, until they were out of sight.

Besides the instant gratification of fun, there was a more lasting benefit to my batting range. I developed a keen sense of eye to pebble contact. Gradually, the strike outs decreased to zero. I never missed. The pebbles flew straight up the driveway - no more yard full of pebbles.

Looking back on my years of baseball in high school, college and beyond, and more years of fast and slow-pitch softball, I hardly ever swung and missed. Best I remember, I never struck out swinging all those years. I had learned to make solid contact there at my batting range.

The batting range remained my secret for the many years it remained in operation - mainly because I didn't want to share the limited supply of pebbles with my friends. It became an afternoon activity I did alone, when no one else was around.

To this day, when I hold a headless ax handle in my hand, I can barely resist the urge to look for a rock to toss up and launch into the upper deck. Fortunately, Lowe's and Home Depot have floors made of solid materials, not dirt and pebbles.

Snipes and Yipes

Probably the only reason I joined Royal Ambassadors at Central Baptist was to go camping. The R.A. program taught boys about world missions, but that had no appeal to my 10-year-old heart. Camping did. We did only one camping trip during my few years in R.A.s, but it was a doozy.

"You ever been snipe hunting?" the older campers asked the new, wide-eyed camper, as darkness settled in, and they added sticks to the campfire.

Having waited for years to go on my first camping trip, I appeared as simple prey for the pranksters eager to pounce. They had sized me up as an easy mark - inexperienced and gullible.

"Snipes? What are those?" I asked, innocently.

"You never heard of snipes?" They could hardly muffle their giggles.

"Tell you what. It's too early for supper, so we'll take you on your first snipe hunt," the oldest R.A. said.

"Great. I'm in," I replied eagerly.

One boy grabbed a pillowcase, and the group led me out into the woods, explaining the process along the way.

"We'll scare up some snipes, and you can trap them in this pillowcase. Snipes are really dumb. They are little, bird-like creatures that run through the underbrush at night when you yell at them. Makes it easy to catch them in the dark."

As we got deeper in the woods, the darkness enveloped us like a thick blanket.

Finally, we stopped, and they instructed me, "Here, Johnny, you hunker down on this trail, and hold the pillowcase wide open. We'll go out there and yell at the snipes, so they'll run your way. Now be sure and turn your flashlight off, so they can't see you. Got it?"

"Sure, guys. Like this?" I asked, crouching down with pillowcase held open and flashlight off. Quickly, they vanished into the blackness of night.

A few minutes later, I heard their shouts from far away, "Shoo snipes! Get outta here! Go, go, go!"

Then silence. I couldn't hear them anymore, because I was back at our campsite. When they first disappeared, so did I, and I hurried back up the trail to our camp. *Yes*, I knew about snipes. They don't exist. And *No*, I would not be fooled by this "green-horn initiation" trick.

I could hardly wait to tell my friend, Shorty Blank, what was happening. He had stayed behind to scavenge for more firewood, but was nowhere in sight. I settled by the campfire with a cup of hot chocolate, awaiting the return of my soon-to-be-shocked and bewildered fellow campers.

Shortly, I heard their comments and laughter as they approached the camp.

"Man, what a dope. He fell for it hook, line, and sinker."

"Did you see his look of terror as we turned away and left him alone in the dark?"

"Yeah, wonder how long he'll stay out there before he panics and runs back?"

"Let's listen. He'll be yelling for us pretty soon."

"Oh man, he'll flip out when we explain to him it was all a joke."

They broke into the clearing, and someone asked, "Hey, who's that sitting by the campfire drinking hot chocolate?"

"Dunno."

"Oh, it must be Shorty, remember, he stayed back."

As they entered the light of the campfire, I turned toward them with a huge grin on my face.

Nonchalantly, I asked, "Where you guys been? Out scaring up snipes?"

Wish you could have seen their stunned, drop-jawed expressions as they exclaimed,

"It's not Shorty, it's Johnny!"

"But you were back...."

"When did you....?"

"How did you get....?"
"Why didn't you....?" they stuttered.

My stock as a seasoned scout rose considerably that night, after I explained to them that I knew about snipe hunting, and how I had sneaked back to camp without them seeing me. They appreciated the fact that I had completely turned the prank around on them.

We sat around the campfire, recounting the story with laughter interspersed often with "I can't believe it."

Then someone asked, "Hey, where's Shorty?"

"Maybe he's still out there looking for firewood," another offered.

We spread out looking and yelling for Shorty, but no response.

Suddenly, I saw something on the ground, picked it up, and shouted, "Hey guys, here's Shorty's flashlight."

Everyone came running as I ventured closer to the cliff shining my flashlight over the edge.

"The cliff?" you might ask. Yes, the only clearing in these woods large enough for several tents and a fire happened to be close to the edge of a 25-foot cliff overlooking a river.

Peering over the abyss, I yelled, "YIPES! Here's Shorty!" He was clinging for dear life to a tree root protruding from the embankment.

With pleading eyes, Shorty could barely gasp, "Heeelp meee."

Lying flat, I leaned over the edge as far as I could and clutched Shorty's hand. The others arrived, and instantly grabbed my legs. I became a human rope. We pulled a grateful Shorty to safety.

While the rest of us went "snipe hunting," Shorty had gone looking for more firewood. Alone in the dark, he had stepped over the precipice, flung his flashlight, and frantically locked on to the root about two feet below. The shock left him dazed, unable to shout for help. That root alone prevented him from plummeting to the rocks below. Not a pretty sight to imagine.

With the gang now complete, we sat around the campfire and imagined that unpretty sight, while eating supper. Several exaggerated re-enactments of the event kept us entertained through the evening. Finally, we retired to our tents, dog-tired from the excitement of our first few hours at camp.

The silence didn't last long. From a tent, someone shouted, "Hey Shorty, go get some more wood for the fire, will ya?"

We burst into laughter again. Then it subsided.

Another offered advice, "Better tether yourself to a tree before you go."

More hilarity. Then silence.

Again, "Get some snipes for Johnny while you're out there."

This continued for half an hour before we succumbed to exhaustion and slept fitfully, dreaming of snipes and yipes.

Boy Scouting - The Camping Years

I graduated from Cub Scouts and became a Boy Scout in the summer of 1953 at age 11. Finally, I could do some real camping, not the sissy stuff like under a sheet in my house, or in my or a friend's back yard. As a Boy Scout, I could now camp in the woods, far away from home, in a tent, among the wild animals, fighting off mosquitoes, ticks, and possibly snakes.

Boy Scouts learn useful crafts, like:
* Making a camp fire and putting out a potential forest fire;
* Chopping firewood and bandaging hatchet wounds;
* Hiking alone in the woods and waiting patiently for the rescue team to arrive;
* Chopping down trees and apologizing to the camper who finds a tree has demolished his tent;
* Cooking our own meals and choking down carbonized bacon, eggs scorched-side up, burned beans, and wieners-flambe'.

The Boy Scout motto is "Be Prepared." I think that advice must have been more for the benefit of the adult Scoutmaster. Camping can be harrowing ordeals for Scout Leaders and parents of young, inexperienced scouts.

I proudly joined Troop 97, which met at the Methodist Church. My first Scout Master, Mr. Hendricks, retired a couple of years after I joined. I hope that had nothing to do with me. A good man and a knowledgeable Scout, he took us camping at the large District campground, Camp Urland, near Woodville, but he never took us out in the woods to rough it alone. He might have been smarter than we gave him credit for.

Our next Scoutmaster, Mr. McDonald, was a camper's camper. He knew how to make the campout an enjoyable, learning experience. After taking us camping to several nearby wooded areas, he persuaded a local land owner to "loan" our troop 100 acres of dense forest, five miles west of Livingston - part of the Big Thicket. That became our regular camp ground for many years. I've asked around for help in remembering the name we gave that site - no one remembers, so I'll just call it "Camp 97." Oh, the memories of those campouts.

Our Troop of 20 boys, ages 11-17, consisted of three Patrols, each with a Patrol Leader, a Scribe, and a Quartermaster. Poor Mr. McDonald was the only adult, but he was tough, fair, and wise - a survivor.

The oldest, most advanced scout served as Senior Patrol Leader. I aspired to become all of those leaders someday, but only made it to Scribe, then Quartermaster. Big disappointment.

On a weekend in November, Mr. McDonald took us on our first outing to Camp 97. Each of the three patrols of six or seven scouts chose an isolated area, and the competition began - to build the coolest campsite.

A friend had brought a 3-man tent, so three of us set it up, while the other four in our patrol set up their two-man tents. Then we dug a small firepit for warmth and cooking, and lined it with stones from the nearby creek. Stepping back, we admired our creation - very satisfying.

Now to go survey our competitors' campsites for comparison. To our chagrin, they were building all sorts of neat things, like tables, and latrines. We felt humiliated and vowed to do better next time.

After supper and troop activities around a campfire, we settled into our tents for a good night's sleep, unaware that a cold front was heading our way. However, as the motto goes, I was prepared. My older cousin-in-law, an Army vet, had given me his worn out, down-filled sleeping bag. The nylon outer shell had several rips, so Mom patched them with electrical tape to keep the feathers from flying out. Let the cold weather come.

Snuggled safely in my Army sleeping bag, I was unaware of the drizzle and freezing temperature that descended that night. When I awoke the next morning, the tent had not leaked, but the moisture inside the tent had frozen. A thin crust of ice covered my sleeping bag.

My patrol-mates were shivering, but I was toasty warm. We had gone to bed fully dressed, of course, so we reluctantly crawled out of our bags and made a fire - a rather large one. That first campout still brings back pleasant memories, believe it or not.

Through the years, we survived many more outings to Camp 97, and our patrol developed a model campsite. We were determined not to be left behind in ingenuity and craftsmanship.

On the second campout, two scouts and I came prepared to make a tarpaulin cabin. I brought my dad's huge tarp, measuring 15 by 15 feet. We chopped down some small saplings, and lashed them together with yellow, store-bought grass rope to form the frame - four walls, gable roof, and front door.

A strong sapling-pole lashed to two trees, six feet apart, formed the roof's ridge and gave stability to the structure. The cabin was about six feet tall, and five by seven on the floor plan, with plenty of room for the sleeping bags and miscellaneous gear of three boys. We draped the tarp over the frame and anchored it with ropes and stakes in the ground. It really looked like a little cabin - a masterpiece to behold.

The other four scouts in our patrol paired up to sleep in two unimaginative, store-bought tents. Together, the seven of us completed our campsite with a dining table with side benches and a cooking table for preparing meals - all made from saplings lashed together.

Our site was near a small creek, so we built a log bridge, with handrails, allowing us to cross over and go visit other campsites. When fellow campers came to inspect our site, they tried their best to hide feelings of jealousy.

On another campout we learned that smart Scouts dig a small trench around their tent to divert rain-water from flowing under the tent and soaking the inhabitants. Too bad we had to learn the hard way.

Most of my camping adventures were "parent approval" rated, meaning I could safely tell my parents what all happened. One misadventure, however, didn't make the rating.

Our Troop 97 joined several other troops in the Trinity Neches District for a weekend camp near Beaumont, Texas. The evening program consisted of scouting-skill competitions inside a rodeo-grounds corral.

Participants demonstrated their abilities, while others waited their turn and observed from outside the surrounding fence. Scoutmaster McDonald and several from our troop were sitting on or leaning against the wooden fence, enjoying the proceedings.

Being a chilly evening, the organizers had placed several smudge pots around the arena for warmth. Yes, I know what you're thinking - space heaters would have been more practical. But remember, we're talking the early 1950's. Smudge pots were "state-of-the-art."

A smudge pot is a small metal pot filled with oil or kerosene. A short chimney on top emits a flame and heat. Sounds dangerous, right? They are. That's why the pot must be placed securely. And they were - all except one - the one closest to our section of the corral.

Gathered close to each other and near the smudge pot for warmth, we alternately cheered and jeered the competitors. Suddenly, we heard a deafening boom, followed by a thud, a crack, and a shriek. The smudge pot had tipped over, plunging its chimney into the loose dirt and formed a pressurized bomb. In a few seconds it detonated sending shrapnel in all directions.

With a loud thud, one huge chunk of metal hit the wooden fence post which Mr. McDonald was standing behind. The post cracked thunderously like a fallen tree, sending a section crashing into Mr. McDonald's torso.

He shrieked in pain and collapsed backward to the ground, lying unconscious. As the smoke cleared, we huddled around Mr. McDonald wondering if he was dead. Finally, he groaned letting us know he could still breathe.

No ambulance was available, so Jim Peters, our Senior Patrol Leader, who had recently obtained his driver's license, borrowed Mr. McDonald's pickup key and drove him to the hospital. An hour later, they returned with a report that relieved our worries. He had only suffered bruised ribs and ego. We could resume the festivities.

Back home I gave my usual recounting of camping happenings to my parents, vividly describing the events, while cleverly omitting some details.

"What's that piece of wood you brought home?" they asked.

"Oh, it's just a section of the post that broke while Mr. McDonald was standing behind it," I explained, giving only the bare facts.

They didn't really need to know about exploding smudge pots, near-death experiences, and emergency hospital visits. Parents, especially moms, don't handle that kind of information well.

I kept that splintered piece of wood in our storeroom behind the garage for many years, as a reminder. Mr. McDonald's wasn't the only near-death experience. Standing unprotected, beside him, I was mere inches away from the shrapnel that shattered that post.

Two tragedies were averted. Neither Mr. McDonald nor I were killed, and secondly, my parents did not forbid my going on future campouts.

Only years later did they get the full report that their only child had narrowly escaped having a jagged piece of metal rip through his body.

As I said, camping can be a harrowing ordeal for parents to endure. It's always best to shield them from potentially disturbing information.

Tornado Trauma

Every time I hear the word "tornado," I cringe and whip my head around to look out the window. It's just an ingrained reflex action over which I have no control. There's an interesting story here.

In my seventh-grade year, we had a tornado alert one afternoon. Teachers and students alike were on pins and needles, because the principal warned us over the PA system that it was coming.

Classes remained in session, but engagement in the lessons lacked intensity. We all focused our attention on the windows lining the west wall of the classroom. Like participants in a horror movie, we fearfully awaited the monster tornado to burst through the wall and devour us.

We knew the drill. If the principal announced, "Exit to the hallway," everyone from each classroom must calmly and orderly file out the door and gather in the long, inside hallway for maximum protection.

I thought to myself, *Yeah, right. Like we're going to do that? It'll be a stampede. Every kid for himself.*

Fortunately, my desk was in the back, second from the door. I primed my legs, ready to spring out the door like a sprinter out of the starting blocks.

The minutes of waiting seemed like hours. As the tension eased a bit, most of the class actually looked at the teacher, Mrs. Sternbranch, if not for education, at least for distraction.

Meanwhile, "Burp" Urpil eased out of his desk and hunkered next to the window, unnoticed. He got that nickname because he could say a seven-word sentence in one long burp. Pretty impressive for us guys - not so for the girls.

The teacher had lowered the venetian blinds and closed them to prevent shattered glass from exploding all over us.

Burp was a prankster. Standing up, he lifted one of the blinds, peeked out and yelled, "Thar she (pause)...ain't!" During the pause, some of us were already half-way out the door, and the teacher wasn't far behind.

"Oh, sorry," Burp said. "I really thought I saw it coming."

A collective sigh of relief filled the emotionally charged room, as we returned to our desks. Heart rates returned to normal, and we resumed not paying much attention to the teacher.

Nerves were a bit more on edge, and Mrs. Sternbranch kept a close eye on Burp in case he had any more shenanigans planned.

"Bitty" Peckerwood, another class jokester, got his nickname from his size - itty-bitty. Bitty didn't really have a plan. The opportunity just appeared, and he capitalized on it.

Rising slowly from his desk in the back corner, next to the window, he grabbed the venetian blinds cord and gave a mighty jerk downward. The blinds crashed loudly as they telescoped upwards. The class levitated - desks and all.

When we landed, Bitty released the cord, loosening the blinds, and a dead fly floated to the floor.

"Got 'im!" Bitty exclaimed.

All but one of us laughed. Mrs. Sternbranch never seemed quite comfortable in our class after that day. Burp and Bitty didn't sit too comfortable in class the rest of that day either. Corporal punishment kept naughty kids mostly in line, and served as a warning to borderline miscreants.

The tornado never came. We were glad, but we sure had a couple of hilarious stories to share and re-enact around school. I wonder if I'm the only kid in that class that still gets alarmed at the mention of "tornado?"

The Big Treehouse

Neither Tarzan nor Swiss Family Robinson could have built a treehouse to compare with the one we planned to build. Eleven-year-old boys have big dreams. Ours was a huge one.

Across the street from my house, stretched a vacant lot. Beyond that, "the woods." That's what we called any unclaimed forest area. "Unclaimed" meant no fence surrounded it - free access.

Most of Poke County was unfenced woods - owned by someone, but ready to be claimed by adventurous boys with big plans for building treehouses or forts, and for practicing their lumberjack skills with the new hatchet their folks had given them with strict instructions not to cut down live trees in the woods.

Cutting down live trees in the woods was fun, and besides it was very necessary for constructing multi-storied treehouses and impenetrable forts. Parents just don't understand things like this.

School was in session, but we had more important things to do. Homework appeared low on our priority list of after-school activities. There were three of us - Willard, Joe Bob, and me.

We all considered ourselves expert treehouse builders, which made it difficult to choose a foreman, so we usually just pooled our lack of knowledge and experience to come up with each step of the design and construction.

We located the tree that would support our treehouse. It was a huge oak with its trunk circumference some ten feet, and its height we estimated must come close to touching the clouds.

First, we needed to collect our building materials. My dad had some lumber and nails left over from building our garage. Joe Bob also donated some used lumber, which his dad had collected from neighbors and delivered to my house.

Next, we needed to transport said materials from my house, through the woods, to the tree. Not the fun part of the project. Our tree was some 300 yards from my house - through the woods. We had learned in school about prison chain-gangs doing forced labor and imagined that we were re-enacting it.

We later calculated that those long two-by-fours and assorted planks must have weighed several tons. Not knowing exactly how much a ton was, we were certain we had handled several of them. After two hours of hauling lumber, we called it a day. The rest of the lumber could wait. Tomorrow we would begin construction.

Tomorrows come at a snail's pace when boys are building a treehouse. Eventually, the final school bell rang, and we hopped on our bikes. My house was about a mile from school, mostly downhill, which suited us fine. I might mention that my morning trips uphill to school, and Joe Bob's and Willard's afternoon trips back home required a lot of leg pumping on our one-speed Schwinn bikes.

Every afternoon that we could work, we carried more lumber on our one trip out to the construction site. Hammers and saws had to be returned to my garage each day for safe keeping. Hatchets were smuggled back and forth secretly.

Arriving back at our enormous tree that second day, we brimmed of enthusiasm. This project would rival Noah's Ark in complexity, if not in significance. But first things first. We needed a ladder to take us to the lower limbs.

Pine trees make excellent ladders, because they are easier to cut than oaks. Our hatchets went to work. Chips flew as we fell two sturdy candidates for the legs. Thinner saplings were chopped into several steps which we tied to the fifteen-foot legs using grass rope. A perfect ladder, even if it was a bit wobbly.

Now it was time to apply our engineering and architectural skills, even though we didn't really know the meaning of those words or how to pronounce them. First, we needed to climb up to the lowest limb and determine where to begin the framework for the first floor of our multi-storied treehouse.

Having enough common sense to not scamper up our rickety ladder all at the same time, we took turns, and ascended to the lowest limb, which was thicker than our three scrawny waists combined. The ground loomed dangerously far below. Looking down twelve feet is a lot further than looking up twelve feet. We were thrilled. This was not going to be your average sissy treehouse.

The lower limbs branched out into smaller limbs the size of only one scrawny waist, which again branched out into even smaller limbs, about scrawny leg size. We needed to locate four
sets of connecting branches approximately equal distance apart to support the four joists of our main floor. My dad had taught us the word "joist" which we used extensively to demonstrate our construction knowledge.

"Hey Willard, measure that joist to see if it's long enough," I suggested.

"OK, joist wait a minute." Willard hadn't quite understood the term, but tried his best to use it. Willard wasn't exactly the Rhodes Scholar among us. In fact, our teachers had correctly predicted that none of us would become Rhodes Scholars. That was fine with us, since we had no idea who Rhode was, and we certainly didn't want to become one of his collars.

With much trial and error, mostly error, we wedged the four two-by-four supporting joists into four forks or "v's" of the lower tree limbs to form a rectangle, the engineer's term for a box. This would be the sturdy foundation for our first floor which would measure approximately six by six-foot, the dimensions being determined by availability of boards for the floor.

Nails and grass rope secured the joists. We hadn't brought a carpenter's level with us, so just "eye-balled" it's levelness. Close enough. So far, we had labored only three days. The rest would be easy, so we thought.

Next, we needed to install a floor. For that, we picked out the choicest planks, since the first floor would be the largest and the area where we would spend the night in our completed treehouse. Concerning our parents, that tidbit of information was classified as "need to know." They had absolutely no need to know our plans until that night arrived.

These floor boards, of course, needed to be nailed securely in place and sawed off even with the joists. Easier said than done. Having no "choice" planks, we picked out the ones with the least knot-holes, splits, splinters, and bows.

The first three floor boards proved the trickiest to install. Leaning off the ladder or hanging from a nearby limb made it difficult to reach the target area with nail and hammer. There were lots of bent nails, "zing" nails (ones that went zinging into the forest by a misguided hammer), and smashed nails - ours.

We didn't know enough curse words at that age to adequately express our pain, but we managed with some we had heard from older kids and made up a few of our own. However, we were stoic about the injury when we arrived home and the excruciation had subsided.

"Oh my goodness! What in the world happened to your thumb?" our moms exclaimed.

Dads usually preferred, "What in the..." their expletives being stifled by darts from our moms' eyes. We almost learned some colorful words to use next time we smashed a finger.

"Aw it's nothing," we lied, holding the mangled digit out gingerly. "Barely noticed 'til you mentioned it."

Somehow, miraculously no doubt, we completed the main floor of the treehouse with no casualties or permanent injuries. It was a masterpiece.

Now for the walls. We saved a few longer boards for the floors on the other two levels of our high-rise treehouse, so we had to use short boards for the walls. The result was that, when the roof was in place, no one over five feet tall could stand up straight in it. This would work great to discourage older, taller kids from commandeering our treehouse.

The walls would need some roof/ceiling joists, and our hatchets were again deployed to the forest. Young pines eagerly awaited their opportunity to become a significant part of the project. Four of them were chosen, chopped, and dragged to the construction site to be installed forming a box somewhat parallel to the floor - about five feet above. Wall construction took several days with lots of sawing, nailing, laughing, and a minimum of mishaps.

"Watch out below. I dropped my hammer." Clunk!

"Hey Joe Bob, what are you doing lying around? Get up and bring me my hammer."

Floor and walls were completed. One side had a door opening, providing access via the ladder. There were windows on all sides for spying out vicious predators - like snakes, wild hogs, wolves, and wild cats, all of which were a threat in these woods.

Girls were also on our security watch list. We had no idea that in a few years, the term "watch list" would have an entirely different meaning in relation to girls.

Now we needed a roof to protect us from rain and other things falling out of the sky or out of the tree's canopy above. More small pine trees were called into service. These we placed across the roof frame at six-inch intervals, nailed them secure, and used the pine boughs to make a thatched roof.

The first level of our epic treehouse was a masterpiece. We celebrated with a snack of Three Musketeers candy bars and bottles of Coke, each costing a nickel. That dime put a significant dent in our measly weekly allowance of one dollar, but this was a significant occasion to celebrate.

Construction of the main treehouse had taken most of the Spring semester of my fifth year of internment at The Alamo. Weather, chores at home, and Saturday afternoon movies at The Fain had prevented us from working every day. Homework interfered also, but we managed to limit its impact.

Summer Vacation arrived before we knew it. Well, not really. We usually began the count-down to Summer Vacation about mid-September. With three months of Summer, we were certain to complete the construction of the next two levels.

Meanwhile, we needed an appropriately impressive name for this magnificent edifice. Calling it simply "The Treehouse" wouldn't do. The Tree Tower and The Forest Fortress were good candidates, as was The Wonder in the Woods.

My dad came out to inspect our handiwork in its early stages and suggested Shade Tree Shanty, or Disaster Dump, or The Oak Joke. I don't think he understood the seriousness of having a noble name for our work of art. In the end we settled on naming it what we had called it from the beginning - "The Treehouse."

Summers are mainly meant for baseball, swimming, and camping. These activities, besides the fact we were running low on building materials, altered our plans for a quick completion of the treehouse. Not quite as much time and care were used in building floors two and three. The structures were similar to the main one but scaled down in size, eye appeal, and sturdiness. Two short ladders connected the three levels.

At last, our triple-storied treehouse was completed. We stepped back and viewed it with admiration.

Joe Bob had a great idea. "Hey, y'all think the Poke County Surprise will send someone out here to take a picture and put it in the paper?"

That's what everyone called the Polk County Enterprise, meaning it would be a surprise if anything interesting appeared in it. Of course, our treehouse never made the front page, but it should have. We would have to be satisfied with the recognition of our parents and, maybe later, a few friends.

We set a day to invite our parents for a private viewing. My mom is the outdoorsy type, so was agreeable. The other two moms would be the hardest to convince.

They complained, "You want us to tromp all the way out in the woods just to see your treehouse? The woods are full of snakes and chiggers and spiders and thorns."

After much begging, screaming, and moaning they finally hushed and consented to come see our treehouse. Our dads were OK with it, and even mildly curious. Dads, previously, were boys. They understood.

So, the next day, a Thursday, we trekked through "that horrible bug-infested wilderness," as two of the moms described it, to the clearing that surrounded our enormous tree and treehouse. Our hatchets had enjoyed denuding the area of small trees and bushes, partly for ease of access, but mostly just for the fun of it.

As we neared the treehouse, our moms exclaimed their "aws."

"Aw man, those briars snared my dress," Willard's mom moaned.

"Aw--aaii, there's a huge spider," Joe Bob's mom shrieked.

In spite of those "aws," they were truly awestruck when the treehouse came into full view. Even the dads were a bit surprised - mostly surprised that their own offspring, who had shown very little enthusiasm about work around the house, could have built such a remarkable structure. We scampered up the ladder, one at a time, of course, and beckoned our parents to join us. Close inspection of the ladder led them to decline the invitation.

"We can enjoy the view better from down here," Joe Bob's dad stated. He knew how to use diplomacy, having served in county government for several years.

Our parents were duly impressed, much to our satisfaction. What better time for the big announcement?

We took a collective big breath, but Willard's mom spoke first, "Well, now that you have that out of your system maybe...."

Willard interrupted her, "Wait, Mom. We have a big announcement."

In unison, we blurted out, "We want to spend tomorrow night in our new treehouse."

Seemed like a reasonable request to us. Willard's mom almost fainted, but thought better about it when she realized she would be lying on the ground infested with chiggers, snakes, spiders, and thorny vines.

Joe Bob's parents enumerated the dangers involved with such an adventure, which included our sleep walking through the open door and plummeting to the ground, or cutting an appendage off of ourselves or each other with our hatchets and unable to get back to my house in the dark, or setting the woods on fire with our camp fire.

That last one gave us an idea we had not thought of - a campfire. Sounded good.

My dad was the most sensible of all and saw nothing wrong with the campout. My mom's suggestion, however, determined the acceptable compromise. We could spend the night under the treehouse, not in it, and absolutely no campfire.

She added, "When it comes bed time, you must be settled safely on the ground, not 30 feet up in the air in that box that could be blown down by a stiff wind."

Oh, well, we weren't going to win this argument, even if it was only 12 feet high, and we had already been buffeted by several strong winds that couldn't even budge our tree or treehouse.

The next day was Friday, T-Day. Our parents had regaled us with World War II stories of D-Day and V-Day. They had survived some difficult years - hard times of which we were barely aware as toddlers. We knew that the stories involved "invasion, occupation, and victory." So, we named that Friday our Treehouse Day, T-Day for short. We would invade, occupy, and have total victory by spending the night *at*, if not *in*, our treehouse.

Sleeping bags and snacks were assembled for the assault. No tent was necessary - we would sleep under the stars. About mid-afternoon we launched the attack. My parents were the only ones to see us off. Looking back to wave at them I noticed Mom wipe an eye. I think a bug had nicked her.

Dad yelled after us, "Y'all watch out for Bigfoot out there." He liked to joke.

Arriving at the site, we set up camp - meaning we tossed our sleeping bags on the ground and began digging into our snacks. Next, we worked on some finishing touches on the treehouse, replacing pine boughs that had blown off the makeshift roof, and shoring up the rickety ladders with more rope.

Soon, darkness fell, so we spread out our sleeping bags and turned on our flashlights, which were a poor substitute for a campfire. What to do in the dark? Well, tell ghost stories, of course. We dredged up some really gruesome ones learned from our friends who were older Boy Scouts. Although we knew the tales by heart, somehow, in the retelling, they became a lot scarier.

Our flashlights conked out early in the evening because we forgot to bring extra batteries. We were in the dark, just the three of us, out in the woods, all alone. Clouds alternately concealed and revealed beams of light from the moon and stars, causing an eerie effect of shifting shadows.

We were terrified, although no one wanted to admit it. The palatable horror of the last ghost story lingered in our minds like a dark cloud as we drifted into uneasy sleep. Actually, there was a dark cloud above us completely obscuring natural light. We were in total darkness.
It must have been around midnight when we heard it. Something was shuffling through the woods, coming closer and closer. We all bolted to a sitting position, still encased in our sleeping bags, eyes open to maximum width, searching wildly in the dark for the source of the creepy swish ... crunch ... swish ... crunch.
Suddenly, Willard shrieked, "It's Bigfoot!"
I honestly can't remember if our ears or just our imagination heard the next sound, but it was definitely the growl of a Bigfoot. Wasting no time to find the zipper, we ripped our sleeping bags open and rushed terror-stricken to the ladder.
Somehow, the ladder managed to accommodate all three of us at the same time as we ascended en masse, clawing and grabbing whatever was available - ladder rungs, frayed ropes, each other's arms, legs, hair, clothing, whatever. Self-preservation trumped over reason or "do unto others."
In a matter of a few horrifying seconds, we were safely inside the treehouse, huddled in a tight, quivering blob of bodies. All fell silent, except for the pounding of our hearts and the gasping for breath. We waited. Nothing.
Gradually, we unfolded ourselves from one another. Maybe our frantic reaction had startled the Bigfoot, and he had scampered away. So, what to do now? We were definitely going to spend the rest of the night *in* the treehouse. We could honestly tell our parents, "Nah, we didn't *sleep* in the treehouse," because we didn't.
Daybreak came about three days late, according to our estimation. When the light was sufficient, we spied out the surrounding woods from safely inside the treehouse. No sign of Bigfoot. We had survived.

Exiting the treehouse was a bit hazardous. The ladder had valiantly sacrificed itself to facilitate our hasty ascent. It would need some repairing, if not total reconstruction.

In the months to follow, we did return to the treehouse a few times, but the adventure had climaxed with that one night we spent not sleeping in the treehouse. We had fond memories of the satisfaction of hard work in the construction of an amazing three-story treehouse.

I've often wondered if, years later, other kids discovered and used that treehouse. Hopefully, they didn't have a prankster dad to put the idea of a Bigfoot in their minds the first night they spent there.

The Teacher Is Here

In Junior High, most of us boys didn't realize our teachers were our friends who desired to educate us. The teachers envisioned molding us into productive little citizens, rather than the hooligans we showed every possibility of becoming. Some of them were strict, but none more so than Mrs. Prongsharp.

She taught Social Studies and, somehow, managed to make it less boring than other subjects we were conscripted to learn. However, she had a bad habit. With a wicked scowl, she often ushered repeat misbehavers down the hall to principal Abel Basher's office for due punishment. It felt like a re-enactment of the Bataan Death March she taught us about in our history lesson. Both marches were scary. Mrs. Prongsharp maintained an admirable measure of discipline in her class.

Besides History, we were inflicted with Geography lessons. To my teachers' amazement, I made all A's and B's through my 12 years of schooling. But the geography portion of this 7th grade class threatened to deal me a C. For some reason I just couldn't get excited about maps, population densities, topography, cultures, and the like. In my adult years I devoured geography ravenously, but in this class, I had no taste for it - except for the globe displayed daily on Mrs. Prongsharp's desk.

Suspended on a half-circle frame with base, the inflatable plastic globe could be rotated for inspection, and it could even be removed - but only by the teacher. We were permitted to gently spin, not twirl, the globe to locate and point to a particular country, but never, never, never to remove it from its frame.

The thought of removing the globe never crossed the girls' minds. The boys, however, would love the opportunity, if for no other reason, simply to do it because it was forbidden. That's how young boys' minds work.

One day, one of our fellow malefactors misbehaved twice in one period. The death march was on.

With offender in tow, Mrs. Prongsharp paused at the door, turned to the class and snarled, "Don't any of you move or say a word until I get back. Got it?" We got it.

Down the hall, Mrs. Prongsharp led the trembling reprobate by his collar to Principal Abel Basher's office. After a short silence in the classroom, the opportunity presented itself.

One guy ran to the desk, removed the globe, and said, "Hey, let's play some basketball."

Another grabbed the teacher's large wastebasket and put it on her desk, saying, "Here, this can be our goal."

One of the brighter guys went to the door and offered, "I'll stand here and yell, 'The teacher's coming,' when I see her heading back."

Great idea. That would give us enough time to replace the globe and wastebasket and scramble to our seats.

Those of us boys actually brave enough (you should read, "foolish enough") divided into two teams and began the game, dribbling the "basketball" and tossing it to one another.

Hilarity broke forth. Even the girls had difficulty keeping their giggles to a low volume. Everyone was absorbed in the game - including the watchman at the door.

Suddenly, he remembered his assignment, and glanced up the hall. Mrs. Prongsharp had heard the commotion, and came hoofing it down the hallway, huffing and puffing, already within a few steps of the door. Judgment day was upon us.

The unfaithful watchman leaped to his nearby desk, sat down, and whispered loudly, "The teacher's HERE!"

Pandemonium broke loose. The basketball players clambered to their desks and joined everyone in appearing innocent and studious. Everyone, that is, except Justin Timer, the last boy holding the globe. He was a good athlete, but not the sharpest tack on the board.

I can still replay my mental video, in slow motion, of those last five seconds and the thoughts going through Justin's head. I just have no words to describe the panic, horror expression on his face.

First, he frantically looked around, right and left, trying to pass the globe off. He thought, *I'll shove it in someone's hands. No, maybe I can throw it at someone. Aw, man, nobody's available.*

Taking a quick step toward his desk, he reasoned, *I'll just sit down and hide the globe. Nah, not a good idea. She'll see it.*

Wheeling around, he took a step toward the teacher's desk, thinking, *If I can put it back in the frame and make it back to my desk. Nope, not enough time.*

Justin had run out of options. Mrs. Prongsharp stormed into the room and glared at Justin standing there wide-eyed, frozen rigid like a mannequin - and still holding the globe. A few snickers broke the silence. This was going to be monumental.

Mrs. Prongsharp walked up to Justin and enunciated, "Put ... the globe ... back ... in its place." He did.

"Go ... back ... to your ... seat." He obeyed.

The whole class, especially Justin, waited for the other shoe to drop. But it didn't. Mrs. Prongsharp continued class as though nothing had happened. That shoe grew heavier and heavier every day, as we waited fearfully for it to crash down with a mighty "THUD!" It never did.

Strangely, discipline was hardly a problem in Mrs. Prongsharp's class after that incident. The boys' behavior was almost exemplary - especially Justin Timer's. We all wondered why Mrs. Prongsharp didn't exact severe punishment on the whole class. She missed a great opportunity to teach us a valuable lesson in proper behavior.

More Boy Scouting

I could write dozens of stories about my Scouting years. But relax, I'll just tell a few.
Boy Scouts of America has changed drastically through the decades. My memories are of the "back then" years when boys were trained to be God-fearing, Bible-believing, morally upstanding, patriotic citizens.
Our Motto was "Be Prepared," and our Slogan was "Do a good turn daily." We pledged "To do my duty to God and my country," and "To help other people at all times." We learned practical life skills which I still benefit from today. From what I hear of the modern changes in the scouting program, I would be hesitant to recommend it.
So, let me tell about some of the "good ole" years. Serious scouts worked with a passion at earning Merit Badges. The green khaki uniform included a wide sash, begging for lots of those 1½ inch round, brightly colored, cloth patches to be sewn on.
Each Merit Badge had an embroidered picture depicting the particular skill attained - Camping, Swimming, Archery, Personal Fitness, Home Repairs, First Aid, Forestry, and Cooking, to name a few. An illustrated booklet for each one instructed the scout how to accomplish the requirements. Each Merit Badge took time and effort. The scout gained skill and knowledge along with each really cool looking badge.
Two or three times a year the troop held a Court of Honor with pomp and ceremony to award Merit Badges and advancements in rank. Parents attended to support their scouts.
Scouts entered the troop as a Tenderfoot and, ideally, worked through the ranks of Second Class, First Class, Star, Life, and, (drum roll), Eagle. Each advancement required a waiting period and a certain number of Merit Badges.

In my six years of scouting, I earned 18 of those coveted badges, attaining Life Scout, just three badges short of Eagle. I still regret not finishing.

Two highlights of my scouting career occurred after my freshman year in high school, in the summer of 1957. The first happened during a five-day district camp at Camp Urland.

Each troop was instructed to choose, by secret ballot, three candidates for the Order of the Arrow - the National Honor Society of Boy Scouts of America. A really big deal. Troop 97 had only one member of this austere organization - our Senior Patrol Leader.

Votes were written on separate pieces of paper and surrendered to the district candidate committee for review and consideration. The results would be announced at the final campfire.

That final campfire was a long time coming - at least in the minds of scouts eagerly wondering, *Who will be chosen? Will I be chosen? What if I'm not? Did anyone vote for me?*

The night arrived. The huge fire blazed, encircled by three rows of log benches to accommodate the 100+ scouts tingling with anticipation. For most, it would be a night of disappointment. But, for a handful, a night of ecstasy.

The songs and pledges were austere and solemn to begin the program. A cloud of reverent anticipation hung over us like the smoke from the fire. Then an Order of the Arrow (OA) leader explained the organization's history, purpose, and importance. Big disappointment. We wanted to know the inside stuff about the secret rituals and mysteries we had heard about.

He ended the oration with details of what would follow - the Call Out Ceremony. Those chosen for future induction into OA would now be "called out," and instructed to come stand beside the leader.

Next, from the shadows, we heard approaching us the slow rhythm of two drums beating alternately - Dum... dum/dum... Dum... dum/dum. Three OA scouts dressed in loincloth, and Indian head dress, with painted faces marched somberly into the circle. Leading the two drummers, the third Indian shook a feather-decorated pole with a rattle on the end, to the beat of the drums.

Suddenly, they paused, the drums beat furiously, and the leader extended his pole toward the face of a startled scout, shaking the rattle vigorously. The scout had been "called out."

The process continued around the circle, until about a dozen OA candidates were indicated and joined the group in the center of the ring. I can testify that each of them was both terrified and thrilled, because, to my surprise, I was one of them!

We candidates returned to Camp Urland two weeks later for a weekend process of Ordeal and Induction. To pass the Ordeal, we maintained silence, survived on small amounts of food, studied the OA Manual to pass an oral exam, and worked on camp improvement projects.

The final night, the leaders said, "OK, boys, go to your tents and roll up your sleeping bags. Meet back here in 10 minutes. Don't bring anything else. You're going on a *real* campout."

We thought, *Great. This will be fun. But why are the leaders not preparing their sleeping bags? Hmm, maybe they already have their stuff waiting at the campsite.*

We hustled back with sleeping bags in tow. Ominously, the leaders handed each of us one match, put a large, green wreath over our heads, blindfolded us, and marched us into the woods tethered to a rope like a chain gang.

One by one they deposited us deep in the woods, far from the trail, and instructed us, "Sit here until you can no longer hear anyone talking or moving in the woods. Then take off your blindfold. You have one match to make a fire and burn your green wreath. Sleep here until morning and find your way back to the main camp."

When I removed my blindfold, I was all alone, like the sole survivor in a tragic wilderness expedition. With only the faint moonlight to guide me, I scrounged around my area for dead leaves and twigs to start my fire, along with a huge stack of small, dead firewood. This conflagration would definitely incinerate my wreath.

Now to light my one match. A less than perfect strike would prematurely end my OA career. Very carefully I flipped the match against the zipper of my jeans. Floom! The match performed perfectly. I shielded the flame with cupped hands and applied it to the leaves. The blaze spread, and soon I had a mini bonfire. The green wreath crackled as the fire consumed it. Success!

Only two requirements remained - survive the night alone, and find my way back to headquarters. Exhausted physically and emotionally, I crawled into my sleeping bag and slept soundly. The hobgoblins and forest creatures must have been sorely disappointed.

Waking at daybreak, I remembered the direction of my entrance and easily maneuvered through the woods, arriving safely where our leaders waited to officially induct us into the Order of the Arrow. They gave us our white sash with red arrow, and, finally, they entrusted us with the OA mysteries, rituals, and secrets, for our eyes and ears only - not to be shared with non-Arrowmen. I'm just itching to tell you some of them, but, as the saying goes, "I would have to kill you if I told you."

My second momentous scouting event that summer was the National Scout Jamboree, July 12-18, 1957. Eight of us from Livingston and 19 other scouts from our Trinity

Neches district joined the 52,580 who converged on Valley Forge, Pennsylvania.

Many highlights come to mind. On the trip there, our train broke down and we spent the night over the Mississippi River.

At the Jamboree, Jimmy Dean and the "Harmonica Rascals" entertained us.

One day, we OA Arrowmen had a special meeting with Vice President, Richard Nixon, who gave a short speech. Several of us got to shake his hand, but we stopped bragging about that on August 8, 1974.

Everyone brought multi-colored camp patches to trade. One innovative Texas scout brought a box full of horned toads to trade for patches. The Yankees were amazed and shelled out stacks of patches for the prehistoric looking creatures.

Boy Scouts of America was a major influence in my formative years. The adventures, the mishaps, the fellow scouts, the skills learned - yep, I'm glad I was a Boy Scout during those glorious years.

You Have a Dentist Appointment

"Don't forget, you go to the dentist today after school," Mom reminded me.
 I cringed in horror - the dreaded dentist appointment. Uncle Judge, Dad's older brother, was one of two dentists in town. His dental equipment was hardly the next step above pliers and jackhammer. His drill sounded like the electric one I now use in my woodworking projects. His dentist chair reminded me of the pictures I had seen of the executioner's electric chair. I can't remember for sure, but I think Uncle Judge had to strap me in.
 His office was a second-story torture chamber above a grocery store. Walking up that narrow passage of steps took forever.
 "Come on, Johnny, Uncle Judge is waiting for you," Mom coaxed. Every step took me closer to a very painful experience. I took my time.
 Cavities were inevitable. I loved the culprits - candy bars and soda water (Cokes, etc.) - but hated the consequences - dentist appointments.
 I sat down and opened wide, heart pounding, eyes bulging in horror. To his credit, Uncle Judge was a gentle man. With a soft touch, he inserted his large hands in my mouth, and poked around using various ghastly-looking, steel instruments to survey the situation. The situation was always grim - there were cavities. I would need fillings.
 He replaced the probing tools neatly on the tray in front of me, so I could view them and recall the pain they had caused. They would return to action later. Then he reached for the ultimate device of agony - the drill.
 Like a caged monster ready to be released for the attack, the drill stretched above, beside, and in front of me. It was huge. There were cables, pulleys, hinged arms, and, of course, the drill bit. The whole apparatus looked menacingly hideous, like a sci-fi robot from another planet. It's good I was strapped in.

Uncle Judge cranked up the drill, and its high-pitched screech scarcely drowned out mine. I'll skip the gruesome part for the sake of the squeamish. Let me just say that a lot of grisly, horrific activity took place inside my mouth.

During the whole ordeal, he did attempt to alleviate some of the excruciation with words of encouragement:

"Oh, sorry."

"Ooo, that musta hurt."

"Just a little bit more on this one."

"Oops."

"We'll take a break. You can relax your mouth and vocal cords, while I adjust my earplugs."

"Only three more to go."

Having excavated several holes in my teeth, some of them to the nerves, he returned the monster to its cage. Now I could spit into the bed pan - that's what it looked like. Maybe it was a urinal. Out came blood, spit, and tiny bits of tooth. If I had been allowed to eat a meal before coming, there would have been more.

Next came the filling - the easy part. I watched while Uncle Judge ground up a dark-grey concoction in a small ceramic cup. With a beefy index finger, he placed a dob of this putty-like substance into each newly bored hole, pressed it down, and rubbed it smooth. No instruments needed.

When finished, he surveyed his work. Satisfied, he unstrapped me, with the instructions to sit still for a few minutes to make sure the fillings dried and set properly. Thankfully, it didn't take as long as regular cement.

The ordeal finally ended. I checked the calendar on his office wall to see how long I had been there. Surprisingly, it was still the same day.

Uncle Judge was my only dentist for the first twenty years of my life. He must have done a good job. Sixty years later, I still have some of those original fillings.

The sequel to this story occurred during my sophomore year in college. I had a sore tooth and feared it meant a cavity, so went to a local dentist. He examined the offending tooth and declared it needed a filling. I recoiled in shock.

"It's just a filling. No big deal," he assured me.

I thought to myself, *Yeah, right. Did you see the inside of my mouth? It looks like a silver mine. I've been through....* I stopped my thoughts with that one - better not express them.

"Well, OK. If it's absolutely necessary," I replied, hoping he would say it wasn't.

I wanted to warn him, "Go ahead and strap me in, for your sake as well as mine," but no straps were visible. We would just have to risk the consequences.

His dental office didn't at all resemble the antiquated, dimly lit, den of horrors I had grown accustomed to. I was surprised and mildly hopeful. Also, a pleasant looking lady stood beside my chair - possibly to comfort me? I found out later her designation - dental hygienist. Uncle Judge probably had never heard of such either.

With his back to me, the dentist busied himself preparing some paraphernalia I didn't recognize. Then, to my horror, he turned and approached me with a syringe. To this day, I can't watch when given a shot. I don't like needles. So, I rolled up my sleeve, turned my head, gritted my teeth, and closed my eyes.

Doctor and hygienist both laughed at what they interpreted to be my attempt at humor.

"Turn around and open your mouth," he instructed.

"What are you going to do with that needle?" I asked.

"This is your anesthetic. It will block the pain," he explained.

I thought to myself, *So, this is the modern update of torture techniques in dentistry. He's going to give me a shot in my mouth! What hideous evils will the dental field come up with next?* I considered bolting out of the chair, driving back to Livingston, and taking my aching tooth to Uncle Judge - but I didn't.

Obediently, I opened my mouth and braced for a lightning bolt of pain. With just a tiny prick of needle and rub of thumb the procedure was over. I had survived.

"I'll be back in a couple of minutes after the deadening has taken effect," he said.

I waited, and sure enough, one side of my mouth went completely numb - no feeling at all. Amazing!

He returned, and I tried to thank him, but all I could manage was, "Shaan yaah"

The poking, drilling, and filling were done with none of the usual accompanying sound effects - from me nor the drill. I could hardly wait to get back to the dorm and inform my friends of the new technique the dental profession has developed to eliminate pain - Novocaine.

Also, I wanted to inform Uncle Judge. This was 1962. Surely, he would be interested in trying out this brand-new marvel of medicine.

I did tell a friend or two, and they couldn't believe it - not that the dentist used deadening, but that I had never heard of it before. Apparently, this astounding news had not yet reached Poke County. I had a mouth full of fillings which had been installed over the years with no anesthesia!

Memories of pain have a way of sticking like Super Glue. They refuse to let go. Now you can understand why I still cringe at those dreaded words, "You have a dentist appointment."

Mauled By A Bobcat

    I apologize ahead of time. If you are squeamish or have a weak heart, you might want to skip this story.
    If you're still here, I will continue. My dad and I went squirrel hunting one Saturday afternoon. As a junior in high school, I owned my own .410-gauge shotgun, of which I was very proud. It had bagged many squirrels, doves, quail, and snakes - and several dove or quail look-alikes.
    Dad toted a 16-gauge pump shotgun that he handled like a pro. He also possessed a 12-gauge shotgun which I enjoyed shooting every two or three months, giving my shoulder time to heal and relocate to its original position in-between shootings. That monster kicked back like a wild stallion.
    Dad arranged for us to hunt on a friend's property in a portion of East Texas piney-woods east of Livingston. His friend, Rastus Heckler, gave Dad the key to his hunter's cabin in case we encountered wildcats, wild people, or wild weather. All three were possibilities. The bobcat, a variety of wildcat, still roamed wild in our "neck of the woods." We were deep enough into the Big Thicket to even encounter the legendary Bigfoot.
    The hunt went well. We would bring eight squirrels home to clean for a feast. Dove, quail, and squirrel are delicious, although the cleaning is not all that much fun.
    Heading back to Dad's pickup truck parked at the cabin, we trembled with apprehension, as twilight suddenly vanished behind dark thunder clouds. A storm was headed our way. We hoofed it to the cabin, thankful for a dry place to take shelter and wait out the deluge. The last glimmer of light faded as I stashed our guns and game in the pickup, and stumbled toward the cabin.
    Now in total darkness, Dad rummaged around in his hunting pack for the cabin key and a flashlight.
    "Hurry up, Dad," I urged him. The thunder and lightning were imminent, and a torrent of rain threatened.

Finding the key, but not the flashlight, he frantically felt around the door handle for the keyhole and, finally, inserted the key. We lunged inside the cabin and slammed the door shut, barely escaping the initial downpour. We were safe, but still with no light.

"Let's find the light switch," Dad instructed. Like two blind people in search of a treasure, we ran our hands up and down the wall and door frame.

"Here it is," I yelled directly into Dad's ear. He jumped back clutching his ear. I didn't know he stood that close.

"Great. Flip it on," he yelled back at me.

I flipped the switch. Nothing happened. I flipped it up and down several times. Still nothing. We were in a pitch-black, unfamiliar cabin with the possibility of unseen wild cats, wild people, and maybe Bigfoot lurking around the cabin, sizing up their prey. Terror gradually grips one's heart like a monstrous claw in these kinds of situations.

"Don't worry. I'll find the flashlight." Dad's words encouraged me. I moved over near the sound of his voice - for reassurance. We were standing side by side now.

"Here it is," he said, and turned it on. No light shined forth.

"What the *&^%$, the *#$% batteries are dead!" My dad never used any kind of bad language around me. I'm just quoting the thoughts bouncing around in our heads.

What now? Dad put his hunting pack back on his shoulder. We stood there facing the inside of a strange, dark cabin not knowing what to do next.

Then all of a sudden, we were back at our house. I will try to recall the sequence of events preceding our teleportation back home.

The downpour was deafening on the tin roof, but the thunder and lightning were waiting for just the right moment. Without warning, the moment occurred. Simultaneously, an explosion of thunder rattled our bones, and a bolt of lightning illuminated the entire cabin. Three feet in front of us appeared a full-size bobcat with bristled hair and bared fangs poised ready to pounce. I rocketed straight up in the air, banging my head on the ceiling. Dad reacted horizontally, hurtling backwards through the door without bothering to open it. I descended with my legs pumping full speed as I hit the floor, leaving skid marks as I exited the empty door-frame. We yanked the pickup doors open, leaped inside, and Dad got more speed out of that truck than we or Ford Motor Company thought possible.

Back home, we took our first breath and spoke our first words since leaving the cabin.

"Hi, Mom. We saw a bobcat a few seconds ago," I elaborated.

"Is that why your eyeballs are bulging and your faces are so pale?" she asked. "And your clothes. Why are they ripped to shreds? Did the bobcat maul you?"

Dad explained, "A thick underbrush full of briars between the cabin and the truck blocked our way. The path around it was too long. We took the short cut."

To be honest, beginning with our reaction at seeing the bobcat, I might have ventured slightly into the fanciful in describing the events that followed. But everything else is solid truth.

We did see the bobcat, and we did share a flash of sheer terror, complete with frayed nerves and pounding hearts. We faced a mounted, taxidermied, full-sized bobcat. In our minds, for one chilling moment, it was live and snarling.

Rastus, a conniving prankster, planned the whole thing. He had removed the light bulb from the overhead socket, so there would be no light, and placed the bobcat just a few feet from the door. We fell into his trap. Back home, after telling Mom the whole story, we all had a good laugh.

Before retiring for the night, Dad and I made sure the bedroom light switches all worked. Neither our clothes nor our bodies were mauled by the bobcat, but our psyche sure bore the marks. I still shudder, even as I tell you this story.

Mayhaws, Chinkypins, and More

"Pass the Mayhaw Jelly, please." Just to say those words makes my mouth water. It's the best jelly in the world, but not the first time you try it. One must develop a taste.

However, the word "mayhaw," by itself, elicits a different reaction. When the jelly is in a jar, sitting on the table, ready to be spread on toast - yummy. But the process to get it there? Yucky.

Mayhaws are small, tart berries resembling cranberries. The trees grow in the moist soil of creek bottoms or swamps of many Southern states, and the fruit ripens in May - thus the name.

Mom was a master mayhaw jelly maker. Dad and I were willing gatherers of the berries, because we relished the outcome, if not the process.

Each May, we three searched the marshy swamps around Livingston where we knew the trees grew. Not having a boat to safely navigate the shallow waters, we donned rubber boots and waded. The ripe berries could be picked from low hanging branches or scooped up, floating on the water, and placed in your plastic pail.

"Sounds like fun," you say.

"Nope," I reply. "It's hard, dangerous work."

"Why's that?" you ask.

"Heat, mosquitoes, wasps, and water moccasins," I answer.

I'll elaborate. May is hot in East Texas. Tromping knee-deep through a muggy swamp, while constantly swatting at pesky mosquitoes is like doing calisthenics in a hot sauna.

Furthermore, you're in the natural habitat of wasps and water moccasins. You must constantly look up for wasp nests and down for moccasins. It will give you whip lash if you're looking in one direction and suddenly hear or feel something in the other direction.

Once I saw a water moccasin swimming toward me and screamed, "Snake!" I materialized on dry, safe ground and heard me yell, "Snake!" I had outrun the sound of my scream. Snakes can do that to you.

Wasps are more difficult to escape - they're fast. It's really funny to watch someone who has accidentally disturbed a nest of wasps. The "disturbees" are murderously angry. The "disturber" is in panic mode, running for his life.

With arms flailing at the attacking wasps, he streaks across the marsh, making huge waves right and left like a motorboat, and leaping over fallen logs in his path. Quite humorous - except if it's you.

Two or three gallons of mayhaws will make plenty of jars of jelly, hopefully, enough to last all year. Easier said than done. In layman's terms, the berries must be washed, boiled, drained, and cooked with a lot of sugar. Mom did all of that. It's a long, messy, smelly process. Not for sissies.

Years later, after I left home for college, Mom was still making the jelly. Poor Dad had the brunt of the gathering duty. I introduced my wife, Diana, to Mom's mayhaw jelly on one of our visits. She politely ate it without grimacing, but soon grew to like it. As I said, you have to develop the taste.

I was already a grandpa before discovering you can buy factory-made mayhaw jelly in the grocery store. I tried some. Umm… OK, but not the real thing. Nothing will ever match my mom's homemade mayhaw jelly.

Chinquapins are another unique, Poke County treat. Various descriptions of this quaint nut from other Southern areas don't match the kind we had. Ours were different, one of a kind - which could be said about most things and residents in Poke County. Our chinquapins resembled a small acorn and grew on medium, oak-like trees. We called them "chinkypins," and they were delicious. Again, you had to develop the taste.

I often came to school with a handful, packed in a pocket of my blue jeans. I tried to be discreet in eating them, but often a friend saw me.

"Hey, where did you get those chinkypins?" he would ask.

I usually pointed east, saying, "Down a country road off the highway, about two miles from here." My words were true, but I deceivingly pointed in the wrong direction.

You see, I had discovered a rare, fruitful chinquapin tree west of town. As a sophomore, I was already driving alone, so had instant access to my secret source of chinkypins. That tree provided me with a generous supply of nuts every time I visited it.

Now for the "more" which I mentioned previously. One summer, I attended a Poke County Wild Meat Festival. Besides the usuals - deer, squirrel, dove, frog legs, rabbit, and crawdads - we enjoyed rattlesnake, coon, wild boar, alligator, and possum. I had hunted and dined on all of the former, but none of the latter.

Being adventurous, I tried a bite of each, and am pleased to report I kept it all down. All of those delicacies had a distinct aroma and taste. I'm also glad to say, "Been there, ate that, and don't care to repeat it."

Once I saw an advertisement for some East Texas cuisines. For instance:
Creamed Possum Garnished in Coon-Fat Gravy,
Armadillo Au Gratin on the Half Shell,
and Skunk a la King.

Didn't surprise me. What did surprise me, later, I discovered it was all a joke. Not that those dishes sounded delicious, and I'm not saying we Poke Countians ate weird stuff. We just didn't mind trying something different - maybe once.

Darkness to Dawning

A familiar idiom tells us, "the darkest hour is just before the dawn." My dark hours or "dark ages" occurred around my junior high (middle school) years.

I was a good Sunday Christian, but not so on the other six days. Back then we guys didn't have many choices of fun, evil stuff to do. Drugs were not available and even alcohol and tobacco were off limits until high school. We had to be creative - and we were. I developed a foul mouth, a bad temper, and poor choices which I couldn't control.

Once, some friends and I were discussing whether we would commit a certain sin. They, too, were good Sunday Christians, and admitted they would not be willing to do that.

I boldly proclaimed, "Well, I would." They were shocked. A frightening conviction surged through my soul like a dark storm cloud, and I knew that this mindset separated me from Jesus. I was lost with no hope of heaven.

During those three or four years of darkness, I made half-hearted attempts to stop the words and choices and activities that enslaved me.

Each time, my friends said, "Yeah, you'll be back. You always come back."

And they were right. My dark ages continued.

However, the dawning approached during the summer after my freshman year. Central Baptist held a yearly Youth Revival each summer, and God spoke to me that week.

I felt as though He said, "Johnny, you have been trying to live for the world and live for Me. You can't do both. It has to be one or the other. Which do you choose?"

I replied, "Lord, you know I have tried to stop these bad habits, but I can't do it. If You can change me, I'm willing to let You."

Confessing those sins, I begged forgiveness and asked Jesus to take over my life. He did. I experienced what Jesus called being "born again."

The following days I told my friends, "I've changed. No more of this stuff. I'm outta here."

They laughed and said, "Yeah, right. You'll be back, just like always."

But this time they were wrong. I never went back. The filthy language disappeared. No more flying into a rage of anger. The poor choices were no longer appealing. Among other things, I quit dancing, which, in my opinion at that time, was a sin.

The dawning came and changed everything. The Lord gave me a passion for evangelism - bringing others to Christ. I began speaking in church and witnessing to friends. The following summers, I organized and led our visitation and witnessing for the Youth Revivals.

As I reflect on those years of my dark ages, I realize that God reached down and snatched me out of a life headed the wrong way. Others continued on that broad path and graduated to alcohol, drugs, broken marriages, and more. I would have been right there with them if the Lord had not rescued me.

The dawning occurred dramatically and decisively, like a sunrise that gives faint rays of light with the promise of more to come. The maturing process would take many more years.

Baseball - My First Love

The count is three and two, runners on first and third, with two outs here in the bottom of the ninth, and Yogi Berra's stepping up to the plate. We've seen quite a pitcher's duel this hot, sultry afternoon, folks. The Yankees and Indians have struggled to score only one run each, and we're headed toward extra innings - if Lemon can get Yogi out. But that's easier said than done. As you know, Yogi's one of the game's best clutch hitters. Oh, wait, here comes manager Lopez to the mound.

(Cheers and boos)

Looks like he's calling for a leftie from the bullpen - it's Newhouser."

(Louder cheers and boos)

We'll take a break while he jogs to the mound and warms up."

(Short commercial break - probably for Wheaties, "Breakfast of Champions.")

Welcome back, fans. Newhouser tosses the rosin bag behind the mound and toes the rubber. He's scowling at Yogi as he looks in to get the sign. Yankee and Indian fans are on their feet."

(Loud cheering)

The tension is like electricity in the air. Here's the windup...and the pitch.

(Crack!)

Yogi swings at an outside fastball and drives it to left. It's a base hit. Here comes Martin trotting in from third for the winning run.

(Wild cheering)

The Yankees clubhouse empties like a disturbed bee hive. They are swarming around Yogi and Billy to congratulate them. It's another dramatic win for the boys in pinstripes.

I loved listening to a baseball game on radio, as a kid. Those announcers recreated the game in living color, right before your mind's eyes. I imagined sitting in the stands, watching all the action, munching on peanuts, and jumping to my feet to watch a homerun sail over the fence.

Harry Caray told hilarious stories and taught me how to sing "Take Me Out to the Ball Game," at the seventh inning stretch.

Red Barber, in his southern drawl, taught me to call a lazy pop-up "a can o' corn."

Dizzy Dean entertained me, as he butchered the English language. "That pitchur ain't got no curve ball," and "He slud into second."

Mel Allen kept me in suspense for several seconds with his "Going…going…GONE!" describing a homerun.

Vin Scully helped me live the game play-by-play, needing no "color analyst" to assist him.

The New York Yankees, my favorite team, won seven World Series during my radio listening years from 1949-1958. My favorite player, Yogi Berra, won three MVP awards during those years. His "Yogi-isms" combined humor and wisdom:

"You can observe a lot by watching."

"It's déjà vu all over again."

"When you come to a fork in the road, take it."

"Always go to other people's funerals, otherwise, they won't go to yours."

And, my favorite, "A nickel ain't worth a dime no more."

Our Sunday newspaper gave a full-page spread of the team standings and individual player statistics. I memorized them all.

When given freedom to choose a book to report on, I always chose a famous baseball player's biography. Too bad baseball wasn't a school subject. I would have aced the exams.

I remember seeing two Hall of Famers at two exhibition games in Houston. At the first, I watched Herb Score strike out opponents with his amazing fast ball. At the second, I watched Stan Musial display his classic swing. After the game, "Stan the Man" sat in the team bus alone waiting for his teammates. I ran up to the window, stuck my baseball up to him, and got his autograph - a treasure that I carelessly misplaced years later.

My bedroom walls gave witness to my love of baseball. Every available space on the walls displayed full-page photos of legendary players, which I cut from magazines - Yogi Berra, Mickey Mantle, Whitey Ford, Hank Aaron, Willie Mays, Roy Campanella, Jackie Robinson, and Ted Williams, to name a few.

Spending money on girls would come years later, so my major budget item was baseball cards. Perry Bros., our local five-and-dime, sold a five-card package plus a card-shaped piece of bubble gum for a nickel.

Those colorful cards, made by Topps, were a thing of beauty. The front displayed the player's picture, autograph, and team logo. The back had his stats and a short biography. During that "golden age" of baseball and baseball cards, I collected hundreds.

Unable to foresee the future value of those cards, I carelessly carried them in my back pocket, used them for "spoke cards" to make my bicycle sound like a motorcycle, and generally used and abused them, storing them in several shoe boxes. Many were autographed, but don't get excited. The autograph was mine - to claim ownership.

Those cards traveled in their shoe boxes with me for 40 years. In Indonesia, my son, Noel, and I often got them out to examine and admire, and I let him take one of each duplicate to college for his personal collection - some 200 cards.

In 1988, he wrote me that his collection was worth about $3000! I quickly discarded the shoe boxes and purchased some sturdy, sealable plastic boxes to safely store the precious darlings.

Well, I started this part of the story, so I better finish it. I took the cards to the States for safe keeping - out of the tropics. For years I attempted to bargain for a good selling price. That's not easy.

Finally, I allowed a friend, a trading card enthusiast, to sell 50 of the most valuable ones for me with the instructions to have the purchase check made out to the Lottie Moon Christmas Offering and mail it to the International Mission Board. I paid a penny a piece for those 50 cards, and the investment had grown to $9000.

The cards I kept are not all that valuable on the market, but they are to me. I still enjoy flipping through the plastic books that now house my collection. I still have my "autographed" Yogi Berra card. Oh, the memories.

Little League began in Livingston the summer of 1952. At age 10, I was the tiniest player on the Yankees, but that was OK. At least I got some playing time and wore the gray and navy-blue uniform of the Yanks.

The other teams were the Phillies, White Sox, and Giants. Best I remember, we Yankees had a firm hold on fourth place in the four-team-league most of my years. I did make the All-Star team my last year.

After my sixth-grade year, four friends and I joined some 100 other boys to spend one month at Ozark Boy's Baseball Camp in Mt. Ida, Arkansas. Coaches drilled us on the basics in the mornings, and we played a game every afternoon. After each game we ran to the swimming lake near the cabins, stripped down to shorts, and "hit the drink" to cool off.

One day a player's father showed up on the field. We could hardly believe our eyes. Allie Reynolds, the famed Yankee pitcher, was in our midst. He gave some tips to the pitchers-in-training, and then offered some advice for hitters.

We whispered among ourselves, "Yeah, right. Like he's gonna tell us how to bat? Everybody knows that pitchers can't hit."

We listened, but had our doubts. Then he told one of the adult counselors to fire his best pitch at him. Butch Brickbone, a former minor league pitcher himself, took the mound. This should be entertaining.

Butch wound up and fired a 90+ mile-an-hour fastball. Allie swung, and the ball rocketed over the fence, deep into the woods, never to be found again. Case closed. Allie Reynolds can hit.

At age 13, I graduated to Pony League baseball on a regulation-sized field and played two years. Baseball had become not just a first love, but a passion. Besides playing Pony League, one year I took the summer job of groundskeeper and umpire for Little League games.

As a freshman I tried out for the high school team. Two years on that team shattered my long-time dream of making the majors.

Fortunately, I had three marketable skills - keeping score, pitching batting practice, and catching batting practice. These are three thankful jobs on any team - meaning, everyone is thankful that someone else will do them, because nobody else wants to.

My dad taught me how to keep the official scorebook with the intricate lines, symbols, numbers, and statistics. Catching, I had learned in Little League, and control pitching came easy after hurling thousands of rocks at trees, telephone poles, and other objects I won't mention.

Seven other freshmen joined the team, and the next year they all became starters. I was first on the "depth chart," but still sitting on the bench keeping score. Coach Grennan Barrett was tough but fair. He had already thrown two players off the team for laziness. I determined to be a hustler, stick with it, and not complain about the injuries I got while catching batting practice. In my short career, there were bruises and torn tendons in both hands.

Prospects for breaking into the lineup were bleak, as I began my junior-year season. We finished non-district play, and the following week began district play - our final five games. I had yet to take the field or swing a bat. At practice that week, coach Barrett announced that Thomas Smith, our first-baseman, would miss a game.

"Norwood, you'll be our first-baseman against Cleveland," he said.

My heart nearly leaped out of my chest. I would be a "starter" - at least for one game.

On game day we rushed to the field for warm ups and to check the lineup posted in the dugout. My name appeared as leadoff batter. I was shocked - so were my teammates. Did coach Barrett see some potential others had ignored?

In the bottom of the first inning, I strode to the plate with my Nellie Fox 33-inch bat, determined to make contact with the ball. That was my strength - just like Nellie. A Hall of Famer, he led the league in singles seven straight years and posted the third lowest career strikeout record - no power, but lots of singles. With thick handle tapering to larger barrel, his bat (and mine) was designed to punch the ball over the infield.

The pitcher glared in for the signal and fired the first pitch. I swung with all my might and blooped a soft line drive over the third baseman's head. My teammates cheered as I raced to first, making the turn to see if I could advance.

Time froze as I tried to soak it all in. *I'm a starter. I hit the first pitch for a single. I can do this!*

My next at bat, I took a couple of balls then drove the third pitch over the second baseman's head - another single. My third time up, I pulled out another weapon I had developed in batting practice - the right-handed hitter's drag bunt. It dribbled lazily down the third base line, and I scampered to first for another single.

Before that bunt, I told the batter behind me to take the first pitch so I could steal second base. He did, and I did.

The key to base stealing is getting a quick jump. I was reasonably fast, but extremely quick.

For my fourth at-bat, the pitcher issued a walk. I ended the day three for three with a walk, and coach Barrett had a dilemma. You can't bench a 1.000 hitter. What to do with me? The next day at practice, he installed me as the starter at second base, my preferred position, and kept me there the remainder of the season. I batted .400 over those five games.

The following year, as a senior, I played shortstop, hit well over .400, and stole second almost every time I reached first. That was a fun year.

And, I might add, I received three letter jackets for my sophomore, junior, and senior years.

To complete the story of my baseball career, as a college sophomore, I became the starting second baseman and leadoff batter for the very first baseball team of East Texas Baptist College. The following year, a case of the flu cut my career short in mid-season, and I never attempted a "comeback."

Baseball has made a "lasting impression" and "left its mark" on me. The following snippets will cause many of you to say, "Oh, that answers so many questions."

When our high school team visited Cleveland for another district game, the pitcher must have remembered me from that first game. He fired a blazing fastball right at my head. Normally, a batter will duck those pitches, but I was looking for a curve, and waited for it to break. It didn't. Wham! Cap, bat, and ball flew in different directions as I collapsed in the batter's box.

"No helmet?" you ask. Nope, not in those days.

Coach Barrett and the team rushed to see if I was dead. I wasn't. It must have been a glancing blow, because the gash was hardly visible the next week, and my cap only needed to be loosened three notches to fit over the swelling.

"I'm OK," I assured the team and the umpire, persuading them to let me stay in the game. No way would I give up my starting position.

Coach Grennan Barrett was already walking back to the dugout, expecting me to get up, shake it off, and continue playing. He was rugged and expected us to be the same. Retrieving my cap, I trotted, albeit, unsteadily, to first base with my first official "hit-by-pitch."

That wasn't my first, or last, conk on the head. I've fallen out of three trees, once knocking myself unconscious.

On another ball field, hearing someone yell, "Look out," I looked the wrong way, and a baseball clobbered the side of my head. It hurt.

After one baseball practice, some guys and I were goofing off in the locker room. I chased one of them around the room with a broom in my hands. Running full speed through a doorway, I unwisely held the broom sideways and clothes-lined myself, extending my body full-length horizontally and crashing to the floor - head first. The injury was almost as painful as the humiliation.

And finally, one non-baseball related incident. On our Senior Trip to New Orleans, some of us were strolling along a crowded sidewalk downtown, gawking up at the tall buildings. I pointed upwards to comment on a particularly impressive skyscraper and walked smack dab into a metal light pole - again, head first. I saw stars and heard lots of laughs.

See? I told you these snippets about "impressions" and "marks" would explain a lot.

Let's move years ahead, to another "love of my life" - Diana, my wife. She also loves sports. She played shortstop on her church high school softball team, which won their division in Dallas. For her first birthday present after our marriage, I bought her a softball glove. Wasn't that romantic?

Through our many decades of wedding bliss we still enjoy watching baseball on TV. The romance continues. We both still love each other - and baseball.

My High School Football Career

Livingston High School's football legacy reaches back to 1916. The team went 1-1 that first year. By the next football season, they reportedly had found a "real" coach, A. E. Gerlach - my uncle. He led them to a 3-2 record, including a defeat of Houston Heights, a team which had gone undefeated for four years. In the following decades, the Livingston Lions picked up fourteen district championships, and a regional championship.

In 1951, the year I entered fourth grade, the Lions won the 2-A District Championship. Then a drought of victories and championships plagued them for almost a decade. I don't think we had a winning football season during any of my four years in high school. And, by the way, none of this can be blamed on me - not my fault. I was never on the team.

I yelled with everyone at the Friday afternoon pep rallies, attended the home-games and some away-games, bought and pinned the ribbons on my shirt and pants. I did everything I could do to create victories, except play on the team - which wouldn't have increased our chances any way.

I loved and played baseball. To do that I would need knees, shoulders, fingers, head, and other body parts that could be painfully and permanently damaged playing football. Besides, I barely tipped the scale at 130 pounds, even on into college.

"What were those ribbons you mentioned?" you ask. Well, every week, the cheerleaders ordered and sold these neat 6x1-inch white ribbons with green print - our school colors being green and white. The ribbons declared vain hopes, like "Go Lions," "Crush Cleveland," or "On to Victory."

We bought these ribbons every Friday at a dear price - a dime each. They sold like hot cakes. Dreamy-eyed girls bought one to impress the football players, or possibly to support the pep squad. We google-eyed boys bought more than we could afford, enchanted by the pretty cheerleaders hawking them.

Sounds like I had no high school football career at all, right? Well, I did. Once as a manager and once as a coach.

First, as a freshman, I did "manage" to get on the high school Junior Varsity football team.

My friend, Horace Trader, asked me one day, "Hey, Norwood, you wanna manage the high school B-team with me?"

I was shocked. Did he mean we would actually train the players, call plays, and make decisions?

"You mean be the coaches of the team?" I asked.

"No, idiot, I mean be the managers - the ones who take care of the equipment during practice and games. We'll get a letter sweater at the end of the season," he explained.

Sounded great. "Sure," I replied, not knowing exactly what this glorious designation, "manager," entailed.

The entailment became clear on the first day of practice. Horace and I supplied the players with water, salt tablets, and sweat towels.

This job is going to be a breeze, I thought to myself. Then practice ended, and we followed the team into the locker room. They shed their sweaty, filthy practice uniforms and deposited them in a smelly heap.

"Now we gotta wash this stinking pile before it ferments," Horace informed me.

We gathered the odorous mass and took it to the wash room, trying not to gag. Fortunately, we had two large washing machines and didn't have to do the washing by hand. It took several loads to complete the job, then we put them in the dryers. The process took more than an hour.

At the end of the season, we had rightly earned a letter sweater along with the players. One minor difference - the big white "L" on our green sweater had "Manager" boldly displayed across the bottom. So what! I, a freshman, had my letter in high school football - albeit, the B-team.

During my senior year in high school, my football career reached its pinnacle. I became the first football coach of the only Livingston Lion to be named MVP in the NFL (Most Valuable Player in the National Football League).

A historical note will help. In 1929 the Junior Football Conference was established to keep idle youth busy and out of trouble. In the 1930s it became known as the "Pop" Warner Conference. By 1959, "Pop" Warner Football had lowered the age limit and the program spread around the country - all the way to Livingston, Texas.

The local organizers decided to have three teams of fifth and sixth-grade boys, and play a round-robin for the first season - the Fall of 1959, my senior year.

They needed an adult head coach and a high school student assistant coach for each team. I volunteered as an assistant and was accepted. Apparently, adequate knowledge of the game - not playing experience - was the only requirement. The three head coaches were battle-scarred warriors - former Livingston Lions with plenty of experience and the old-football-injuries to prove it.

On the first day of practice, we six coaches observed the wannabes demonstrate their skills. Then, we held the First Annual Draft of Livingston's "Pop" Warner Football, which we nicknamed "Pee Wee Football." Some 50 eligible peewees, of varying sizes and ability, lined-up on the auction block, hoping to be chosen early. Most of them looked like little life-sized bobbleheads with large helmets and tiny bodies.

I had some inside information, because I knew most of the boys. The least likely looking athlete out there, Adrian, was the most talented and a straight-A student. We chose him first, and made him our quarterback.

Next, we chose the biggest kid, nicknamed "Little Boy." He tipped the scale at about 160, heavier than some of our high school linemen. We set him at center, where he formed a one-man wall for Adrian. These two were our co-captains.

The drafting continued, and after several picks, we took Mark Moseley, an unknown, since his family had only recently moved to Livingston. I knew him, because his family were members of our church. He was built like an athlete, so became our fullback. Mark was destined for heroism, as I'll explain later. The draft ended after each team chose 13 players, probably because the sponsors could only afford full equipment for that many.

Football plays were fairly standard in those days. The "Shotgun," the "Option," the "I-formation," the "Wildcat," and the "Wishbone" were innovations awaiting future discovery. The Lions and most small-town high school teams still used the basic formation - quarterback behind center, left and right halfbacks a step behind and a step to the side of the quarterback, and fullback two steps behind the quarterback. Plays were basically handoffs to one of the backs who attempted to squeeze through a hole in the defensive line, or scoot around end. Passes were rare.

Armed with this rudimentary understanding of running plays, I was designated the offensive coordinator of our Pee Wee football team. Adrian, our savvy co-captain, helped me teach the system to the team, and he took control on the field.

One day at practice, I taught the team a "secret play." The center hikes the ball between the quarterback's legs directly to the fullback. The whole team then takes off running to the right. The fullback, with ball wrapped hidden in his arms, takes a step to the right, pauses, then sprints to the left.

Hopefully, the defense will pursue in the wrong direction, leaving the field clear for the fullback to streak down the sideline untouched and score a touchdown. Worst case scenario, the defense responds slowly to the misdirection and is waiting en-masse, like a pack of hungry wolves, to devour the unprotected fullback. I instructed Adrian never to use this play unless I called it.

The season was planned to last three weeks, but lasted four. The three games of round-robin were played on Friday afternoons on the elementary school ground, which was small - the right size for Pee Wee football. Our team soundly defeated the other two, while one of them defeated the other.

We reigned as undefeated champions for the short season. Victory is sweet. However, the other coaches were not content. Anything less than victory is sour. They wanted satisfaction, if not revenge, so devised a plan. A final championship game would be played between our team and an All-Star selection from the other two teams. We accepted the challenge.

They scheduled the game for the next Friday, to be played on the high school football field an hour before the Lions kickoff. A huge crowd of fans would attend.

When we took to the field for warmups that night, players and coaches were "pumped," although we didn't know to call it that. We probably said "revved-up" back then. We were also a bit awestruck. This regulation field could hold two of our elementary playgrounds with room to spare. We wondered if our small players could actually move the ball the length of that huge field for a score.

Since our offense was a well-oiled machine, I took time to sharpen-up our defense in preparation for the epic battle. Also, I reminded Adrian that we might need to use our "secret play" at some point in the game.

Kickoff time arrived. None of the pee wees could kick the ball farther than 30 yards, so the team who won the toss lined up their offense on the 20-yard line to begin the game. That 80-yards to the goal looked like a mile.

The game provided a lot of excitement, as parents cheered enthusiastically for their future stars. The players fought valiantly chugging up and down the field in their comically oversized football gear. But regulation time was running out, and neither team had scored. The kids didn't care. They were having fun.

About one minute remained on the scoreboard clock, and we had the ball on our own 40-yard line. We had 60 yards to go and time for one more play. I signaled Adrian to call our "secret play." The team huddled as the clock ticked away the seconds.

Adrian took extra time in the huddle to explain the play. "OK, men, listen up. We're going on the count of three. 'Little Boy,' you hike the ball between my legs directly to Mark behind me. Everybody run like crazy to the right. Look at me! Right is that way," he said, pointing in the intended direction.

"Mark, you know what to do. Good luck." It all sounded rather ominous to Mark, but he steeled himself for the task.

The clock showed 15 seconds when Adrian brought the team to the line. The players took their stances, and Adrian shouted, "Hut one...hut two...hut three." The ball sailed between his legs, directly into Mark's waiting arms. Our ten players took off to the right like a heard of spooked horses, or, as in this case, wobbly-legged ponies. Eleven defensive players chased them on cue.

Mark hesitated a moment, and found himself all alone, securing the football out of sight. The "secret" play was working. Mark streaked down the left side-line, untouched, 60 yards for a touchdown.

The high school student assistant coach hoofed it down the left side-line, cheering him on to the winning score. The crowd went wild. The other team and coaches stood stoop-shouldered and stunned. Time had run out, and we won the game 6-0.

Mark went on to be a star quarterback and place kicker as a Livingston Lion and a Stephen F. Austin Lumberjack. He was drafted into the NFL as a placekicker for kickoffs, extra points, and field goals. In 1982, as a Washington Redskin, Mark was voted MVP in the NFL. He's the only player to win that award as a "special teams" player.

152

I'm rather proud of my input into Mark's early development as a football super-star. However, I can find no mention of me in a Google search of his career. Just goes to show you that you can't believe everything on the internet - they tend to leave out vital statistics and amazing information.

By the way, after I graduated, the Lions won three consecutive District Championships, 1961-1963. Again, not my fault.

Central Baptist Church

The words "Central Baptist" conjure up a hodge-podge of memories - some religious, some ridiculous. As I shared previously, Mom, Dad, Butch, and I were faithful church members. I remember advancing through the Sunday School departments: Beginner, Primary, Junior, Intermediate, and Youth. We were enrolled by age, so at promotion time, I was often left behind while some of my older friends, though of the same grade in school, advanced to the next department. Very humiliating.

My most embarrassing moment in Sunday School, however, happened in the Youth Department. You have to picture the setting. On Sunday mornings, some 30 youth gather in a large room for "assembly" before dividing into several boys and girls classes. The only entrance door to the room opens just a few feet from the speaker's stand in the front, where the Superintendent stands to give a welcome. Late comers try to sneak in quietly. Remember that teenagers are self-conscious and make every effort to appear cool.

Not realizing the assembly had begun, I flung the door open and rushed into the room, causing everyone to immediately focus on me. In that instant, a fly decided to land directly on my nose. Startled, I swatted viciously at the fly and landed a solid punch to my nose. Blood spurted out. Not cool.

I groped for my handkerchief with one hand while trying to stop the gush of blood with the other. My grand entrance "brought the house down." I repeat - not cool. Kinda hard to nonchalantly stroll to your seat in such a situation. Finally, the laughter subsided, only to be revived as several wise-crackers suggested some hymns.

"Hey, let's sing 'When I See the Blood.'" More laughter, then a brief calm.

"How about 'Nothing But the Blood.'" Louder laughter.

Suddenly, an adult leader stood and reprimanded, "Hush. Y'all should be ashamed of yourselves."
Indeed, we should. Teenagers can be so sacrilegious. You guessed it. I was laughing right along with them, even trying to think of a hymn to suggest myself.

We had some great pastors during my years at Central. All respected men of God who shepherded the congregation with love and wisdom.

Ben Welmaker (1946-1950) left Central to be a missionary in South America. I missed his son, Benny, one of my best friends. I feared that Benny would be devoured by man-eating alligators or captured by monstrous gorillas. Or worse, swallowed live by a giant anaconda. My understanding of the "mission field" was limited to what I had seen in movies.

Vester Wolber (1951-1955) must have studied medicine before becoming a pastor, because everyone called him "Dr. Wolber." I don't think he had a doctor's office anywhere, though.

Wade Hopkin (1955-1959) had a son my age - Scott. We met up again as fellow students at East Texas Baptist College.

James Garrett (1959-1967) pastored during my last year of high school and my college years, when I became a more serious Christian. "Brother Garrett" was a friend and mentor.

These pastors must have been well-educated preachers, too, because I can't remember understanding much of what they said. As a youngster I would wake up every so often and try to pay attention.

As an older youth, I occasionally disengaged from whispering with the friends sitting around me and focused on the sermon. But it took too much effort. I got the impression that sermons were for adults, and only they were supposed to be able to comprehend.

Central Baptist Church has an interesting history. Being organized in 1847 as Ariel Baptist Church, it was renamed to Livingston Baptist around 1865, and to Central Baptist in 1917. But in the beginning, they had no building in which to meet. The Methodist constructed the first church building in Livingston a few years after their organization in 1849.

The Methodists shared their building with the Baptists and Presbyterians. The three congregations took turns leading the worship service, and seating was segregated, with women and children on one side and men on the other. Baptisms were held in nearby Choates Creek, which also served as a swimming hole.

Eventually, the three congregations erected their own buildings. Livingston Baptist built a small frame church house, in 1882, on the land adjacent to the original Methodist building.

A church split occurred in 1904, when First Baptist Church formed and relocated. Two years later, the members who remained at Livingston Baptist replaced their building with a red brick church costing about $4200. In 1917 they changed the name to Central Baptist Church.

The site of the original Methodist building is now occupied by the Old City Cemetery. I wonder if any of their members knew they would spend a long time on, or in, that plot of ground.

The Old City Cemetery is now an official Historic Site covering one full block across the street from Central Baptist. The last interment occurred in 1940. That plot of land gave birth to Livingston's first church building, and eventually received the burial of some 300 Livingston citizens.

Now to test your memory. Earlier in this book I told the story of my church-planting great-grandmother, Arabella Norwood McCrorey. Remember? What?! You skipped over that part? Well, bear with me, we'll just have to review.

Arabella married my great-grandfather, William Norwood, and gave birth to my grandfather, John E. Norwood. William died three years later, and Arabella started the first Baptist Sunday School in the Tempe area, which grew into a Baptist Church, near Livingston. Some years later Arabella remarried Rev. Thomas McCrorey.

"The point being?" you ask.

In the process of researching and writing these paragraphs, I have discovered that Arabella's two husbands, William Norwood and Rev. Thomas McCrorey, are buried in the Old Livingston Cemetery.

On Rev. McCrorey's brick vault is written:

"Calm on the bosom of thy God,
Fair Spirit rest thee now,
Even while with us the footstep trod,
His seal was on the brow.
Dust to its narrow house beneath,
Soul to its place on high,
They that have seen thy face in death,
No more may fear to die."

Now that's a rather touching tribute, isn't it?

But wait. There's a shameful part. My friends and I used to sneak into that unkempt graveyard to play hide-and-seek and to peer into open graves. In some, we could even see parts of a skeleton. Creepy. I just hope I wasn't viewing my great- grandfather's bones.

For younger readers who would like to go examine for yourselves, forget it. The Old City Cemetery is now enclosed with a decorative iron fence, and beautified with oak trees and wild blue bonnets. In fact, it is number five in Trip Advisors' list of "15 Best Things to Do in Livingston." Which fact might also discourage you from even bothering to visit Livingston at all.

At least there are now 15 things you can do in Livingston. In the 40s and 50s our list would have looked quite different - and shorter.

I looked forward to Sunday evenings at Central. We had Youth Choir at 5:00, a quick sandwich supper at 5:45, and Training Union at 6:00. For Worship at 7:00, our Youth Choir sat in the choir loft and performed the special music we had learned earlier at practice. A piano and organ were our only accompaniment.

A confession - I could not carry a tune. (Remember my story "Disastrous Duet?") My friend, Charles Ray King, had a bass voice and sang the melody one octave lower. Perfect. I sat by Charles and tried to follow along, sometimes just lip-syncing to avoid embarrassing myself - and the rest of the choir.

Being a fairly accomplished choir, we got invitations to perform in other churches. In fact, we performed once on the newly founded TV station, KTRE in Lufkin, Texas. The TRE part of the call sign refers to the heavily forested geography of Deep East Texas – TREes.

Summers meant Youth-Led Revivals. Weeks of preparation led up to a full week of meetings. A youth evangelist and song leader were invited, and we organized our own committees - hospitality, advertising, fellowships, and visitation.

During my last two years of high school and first three years of college, I was chosen to head up the visitation/evangelism committee. We collected names of friends who were not enrolled in another church and visited them at home, inviting them to the evening services and attempting to share the gospel.

A lot of "conversions" occurred during the altar calls each evening - mostly young backslidden Christians converting to a more committed walk for Christ. Poke County was dry, but beer was available elsewhere.

Immediately after a Youth-Led Revival, attendance decreased at the joints across the county-line, and increased at Central Baptist – at least for a while.

Advertising became the most popular committee activity, with plenty of volunteers. We got permission from the Sheriff's Department to whitewash downtown streets with announcements about our revival services. It had to be done after midnight to avoid traffic. Yeah, like there would be heavy traffic through Livingston at night? I think, in the years I participated, we had to stand aside only once for a car passing by. Hmmm, wonder what that driver was doing driving through Livingston so late at night?

With paint brushes and cans full of whitewash we covered the main streets of Livingston - both of them - with information and slogans about the services. Several teams painted arrows for different routes leading to Central. I'm not sure it increased the attendance, but it sure was fun to do.

Central Baptist heavily influenced my formative years. I'm thankful for Sunday School teachers that didn't give up on me, deacons that didn't excommunicate me, pastors that didn't ignore me, and friends that encouraged me to join them in following our parents' advice to "get out there and make something of yourself."

My High School Teachers

We'll begin with a few disclaimers. First, concerning teachers' names, I made a unilateral decision not to reveal their names. I ain't no dummy. If you think you recognize any of them, just keep it to yourself.

Also, let it be known that I really did love and respect all my teachers. They molded me - chipping away relentlessly and patching where needed. I'm thankful they saw a potential.

Finally, these stories are true. I report them with no fear of indictment, because the statute of limitations has long passed.

OK, so I'll break my own rule by naming my favorite teacher - Mrs. Verna Garner. A dear Christian lady and adult Sunday School teacher at Central Baptist, she taught my favorite subject - Math. Under her tutelage, I fell in love with Algebra, which led to a love of Trigonometry and Geometry. She made it fun. Besides that, she read us a Mother Goose nursery rhyme once a week from a book that explained the origin and political meanings behind each rhyme. Very thought-provoking.

One day, my friend, Alvin Grindstone and I were in the restroom hurrying to get to Mrs. Garner's class.

Frantically struggling to zip up his pants, Alvin said, "Norwood, my zipper is stuck. Tell Mrs. Garner why I'm late, but don't tell anyone else."

"Sure, no problem," I replied.

You can probably guess the rest of the story, but I'll tell it anyway. I hurried down the hall and stepped safely into the classroom just as the bell rang. Going directly to Mrs. Garner's desk, I informed her of Alvin's problem and took my seat.

"Hey, pass it on," I whispered to several classmates close by. "Grindstone is in the bathroom with his zipper stuck." Juicy news like that travels fast.

Mrs. Garner began class. We waited. Soon Alvin walked in - rather red-faced. The class broke into cheering and clapping, spiced with a few ribald comments. Alvin glared at me in anger. Mrs. Garner glared at me, but with a slight, twitching grin. I responded to both with a "Huh, why are you glaring at me?" expression.

The story spread for years, and became part of our senior class lore. Alvin gained a new nickname - Zip.

Another favorite teacher was Mrs. Trenchcoat. She maintained discipline and commanded respect in an acceptable way to us teenagers. We knew the limits, but were always testing them.

Once she jokingly said to the class, "The next page in your text is not important. You can just tear it out."

No one questioned her. We knew what she meant - and didn't mean. Quickly, I yanked a piece of paper from my notebook and ripped it to shreds. Laughter erupted. Even Mrs. Trenchcoat had to cover her mouth to stifle a giggle.

When the laughter subsided, Mrs. Trenchcoat said, "Now class, you know that was not really a page in his textbook." More giggles. "He's just trying to show off." To her credit, I believe she appreciated my humor - sometimes.

Another time, she said, "OK, class here's a reading assignment to keep you busy while I take these papers to the principal's office"

I wondered, *Surely those aren't a list of her accusations and complaints about my behavior. Nah, the stack is too thin.* She stepped out of the room, and I uncharacteristically applied diligence in quietly reading the assignment.

As the minutes went by, the discipline deteriorated. Like a tidal wave building from a small ripple, whispering grew to a loud rumble. Soon the class erupted into an uproar. Mrs. Trenchcoat materialized at the doorway, and the uproar silenced.

Looking directly at me she growled, "Alright, Norwood, what did you do?"

I stammered, "But, Mrs. Trenchcoat, I didn't do anything. I've been reading the assignment you gave us." And it was true. For some strange reason, I had not joined in the ruckus.

I could hardly believe it. The class could hardly believe it. I was actually innocent - this time. Mrs. Trenchcoat couldn't believe it either. In fact, she probably never accepted that fact.

Next, let me introduce Mr. Sternfast. He frightened us, hardly ever smiling, and never attempting to be our friend. At least that's how we perceived him. I wish now that I had tried to get to know him and some other teachers, who probably would have welcomed the opportunity to be viewed as a person with more to offer than just information and grades.

Mr. Sternfast did make one effort to relate to us outside of academics. He offered a fascinating physical challenge to the class.

Standing in front of his desk, he said, "Which of you boys thinks you're the strongest one in class? Let's see if you're stronger than me."

We all looked at Jibber Grizzley, the most muscular and athletic among us, and coaxed him to step forward. He did so, with a mixture of confidence and apprehension. We wondered what would happen. Jibber wondered what would happen.

Mr. Sternfast directed him, "OK, Jibber, stand beside me, facing the class, with arms extended like this." He stretched his arms out sideways, and Jibber did the same.

"Now rise up on your tiptoes and hold steady." Mr. Sternfast demonstrated, and Jibber followed. We watched as teacher and student stood spread-wing, elevated on tiptoes.

"Don't move now," Mr. Sternfast instructed. "Stay as still as you can, in this position, for as long as you can. Let's see who can do it the longest."

This was getting interesting. Of course, we cheered and encouraged our classmate, confident he could win. But, after about a minute, Jibber began teetering. Another 60 seconds and his arms alternately sagged and rose again resembling a large, clumsy bird slowly attempting takeoff. His calves were burning now, causing him to slightly bounce up and down, as he tried to maintain balance without touching heels to floor.

Meanwhile, Mr. Sternfast remained in form, like a statue, completely rigid. We began laughing at Jibber and cheering for Mr. Sternfast. Jibber lasted about three minutes, if you count flapping arms and tiptoeing back and forth to remain aloft. Finally, he collapsed in defeat and returned to his seat, quite humiliated.

Mr. Sternfast held his stance another minute, never tottering, and addressed the class. "I practice this every day, plus some other exercises. Jibber, you don't need to be embarrassed. It took me a long time to be able to do this. You did good."

That was a 50-something year-old man talking to a teenage jock. Very impressive. We had a new respect for Mr. Sternfast.

I will break my rule again and name a teacher, because the following story will identify her to most of my classmates. Mrs. Manley, another of my favorites, was demanding. She taught History with a passion and expected us to learn it, willingly or not. To pass, we had to memorize historical dates, names, locations, and events, and write reports on them. The final test was a doozy - no picnic for the lazy or faint-hearted.

She also required us to write a 10-page term paper with footnotes and bibliography. Let me explain the word "write." In 1959, personal computers and the internet had not even reached science fiction stage. We're talking hand written, in cursive script, with refillable ink pens, on three-holed lined paper.

"Delete" meant if you make a mistake, rip it up and start over on a fresh sheet. "Save" meant keep a completed sheet safe and secure, because if folded or smudged it would have to be "deleted."

"Spell check" meant look up any word you're not sure of in the dictionary. "Research" was done in the library with real books which you "search" for in a card catalog.

From Mrs. Manley, I learned how to study and retain information. I aced that dreaded final exam with a 97, and got an A+ on my research paper. Mrs. Manley probably did the most to awaken our interest in her subject and prepare us for college.

However, some of us discerned that she was not all that demanding discipline-wise. We smuggled snacks into class and passed notes secretly, never getting caught. Looking back, I think she probably knew, but ignored it.

Sometimes she left us unattended in the class and disappeared somewhere down the hallway. In her rather large shoes, her footsteps clacked loudly on that hard wooden floor, so we could always tell how far she had gone, and monitor her return to the room.

Once she burst into the room and scolded us, "I could hear you talking all the way down the hall!"

A smart-aleck replied, "Yeah, and we could hear you coming all the way down the hall."

We all got a good laugh out of that - all except Mrs. Manley. I think that guy made a C in History, fortunately.

Mrs. Manley's large wooden desk was something of a monument - unique. From our view point, it had a solid back. From her viewpoint, it had a drawer and bookshelf on both sides, with an open space between them for her roller chair and legs.

On the surface of the desk, she neatly arranged a stack of books, a pencil holder, a tray to receive written assignments, and an odds-and-ends tray for paperclips, erasers, and new chalk.

"New chalk!?" you ask.

Yes. The wall behind her desk held her power point system - a blackboard or "chalkboard." It had a wooded tray along the bottom to collect chalk dust and to hold slightly used chalk, and several erasers. The erasers were slightly larger than modern whiteboard erasers and often needed to be taken outside for a good banging to clean them. The whole system was quite messy.

After returning to the room, or after standing to write on the chalkboard, Mrs. Manley commandeered her desk with a flourish. Sitting in her office chair, she dramatically rolled her legs under the desk and resolutely positioned her elbows on the desktop, ready to speak wisdom to young minds. It was rather dramatic.

One day, Mrs. Manley gave us a reading assignment on the adventures of Lewis and Clark. She left the room, and wound up all the way on the other side of the building. This we knew by the sound of her footsteps. Several of us had waited for just such an opportunity.

We nodded at each other, jumped up, and ran to her desk. Carefully, we turned the desk backwards, so the open side faced the class, and the solid backing faced her chair. Then we reversed the objects on the desk to appear in the same order she had left them.

The chair remained in its place, ready for her to plop down, and attempt to roll herself up under the desk. Everything looked normal. We hustled back to our seats and waited.

The anticipation mounted like the rumbling before a thunder storm. By then, some of us began wondering, *Was this a wise thing to do? She could really get mad and punish us severely.*

But we also reasoned, *Nah, she'll see the humor and laugh along with us.*

Soon, the telltale footsteps announced Mrs. Manley's approaching return. The pins and needles upon which we gingerly sat got sharper. She burst into the room, pleased to have heard only silence on her trip down the hall. Going directly to the chair, she parked herself in it and began inching toward the desk while expounding on the dangers and difficulties faced by Lewis and Clark.

Four sentences into the lesson, her knees bumped against the back of the desk, and a slight frown furrowed her brow. Without hesitation, she continued her lecture, while slowly backing up. She gave it another try from a different angle. Bump again.

This continued for several approaches and several bumps. Mrs. Manley was having more trouble rolling up under her desk than Lewis and Clark crossing the Rocky Mountains. A looming explosion of laughter built up like an over-inflated balloon.

Mercifully, the bell rang, and the culprits hastily escaped the room. Mrs. Manley remained unaware of what had happened.

We learned later that the next class helped her rearrange her desk. Apparently, she could not determine whether our class or the one before us had committed the sabotage. We perpetrators were happy to keep that a secret.

To repeat, I respected and appreciated all my high school teachers. Each one expected more of us than we thought possible. They were tough on us for a purpose - to inspire us to achieve.

I suppose they had to be especially strict toward certain scoundrels among us. I could tell you some of the outrageous things a few classmates did, but you might erroneously think I was involved personally.

TIDBITS THROUGH THE YEARS

Gertrude and Neelie

It's difficult nowadays to speak the truth and "tell it like it really happened," for fear of offending someone. In writing, you are expected to conform to the correct vocabulary, and even change history if necessary. I can't do that. Here are the facts as they occurred - written in the vernacular.

The 40s and 50s were the days of non-violent segregation in Poke County. As far as I know, we had no Ku Klux Klan (KKK). Blacks were in the minority in Livingston and lived in their own subdivision with their own public schools.

Most stores and public buildings were open to everyone, with one exception - The White Kitchen café was intended for only those described in the name.

Indians from the nearby Alabama-Coushatta reservation attended Livingston public schools, as did Hispanics. There were no marriages between the races.

Was there prejudice? Yes, from all races towards the other races. Was there "hate speech?" Yes, again, from all groups. There were slurs and derogatory names used by all groups towards other groups different than their own.

I grew up hearing and, regrettably, using those names. Everybody did it. During my high school years, however, I grew aware of the harm and evil of prejudice and ethnic slurs. When I made my views known, a close friend called me a "_____-lover." I took that as a compliment.

You'll have to wait for my next book, to learn about my college roommates – an African American, a Mexican, a Samoan, and a Fijian. I will also tell about almost being fired from a church staff for bringing blacks into our church, and about how my wife and I lived among South and Southeast Asians for 35 years.

Now for the stories about Gertrude and Neelie. During my fourth-grade year, my mother was offered a job as an office secretary at the courthouse.

"What about Johnny?" she asked my dad. "What will we do about him?"

"I've been asking that for nine years," Dad replied.

They had a good laugh.

Mom continued, "No, seriously, can we hire someone to clean the house and keep Johnny after school?"

"I suppose we can hire a maid," Dad offered.

Let me explain about Dad. He was prejudiced, yes. Being a product of his upbringing in Livingston, he used all the racial slurs, but never in malice. He befriended and hired several black men for odd jobs, paying them a fair wage. I learned from him to treat every human being with respect and fairness.

Enter Gertrude - our black maid. She was a good house-cleaner, a fair cook, and a friendly babysitter (I didn't like that term - it was demeaning). A year later, we moved to the house on Calhoun. Exit Gertrude. She found another job.

Mom also changed jobs. We needed another maid/housekeeper/cook. I like to think that my folks figured I was old enough at 10 years to no longer need a babysitter.

Hopefully, they could trust me not to burn the house down or injure myself too bad if left alone after school. Or maybe we were still too poor to hire a full-time helper. Whatever the case, they hired a delightful lady, who endeared herself to our family for the next 25 years - Neelie.

One of her children brought her to our house in the mornings around 7:30, and Dad gave her a ride home after lunch. She cleaned the house, washed clothes, and cooked lunch. I'm guessing she could outcook all the helpers in Livingston.

In all my travels I still have never tasted the equal to the delicacies she prepared. The aromas linger in my memory - blackberry and peach cobblers, apple and cherry pies, fried chicken, and mashed potatoes - all to-die-for. She also knew how to make spinach so even I liked it. My plate was off-limits for all other veggies.

Neelie worked alone in our house each Monday through Friday morning. We never locked anything, trusting her completely, and she proved trustworthy. Being a good Christian woman, she must have been very relieved, and maybe a bit proud, to see me survive junior high and high school, finish college, get married, and have our three children. I wonder if she and Mom ever discussed Mom's prediction that I would become either a criminal or a preacher.

At lunch time we sat around our small kitchen table. There was room for Neelie, but she declined the invitation. We would have been OK to have her eat with us, but she insisted on sitting just outside the kitchen door, some six feet from the table.

She did join in the family conversation, offering humor and words of wisdom. Afterwards, she cleaned the table and ate her lunch alone.

Fast forward some years later, after Diana and I became engaged. On her first visit to our house, Diana was amazed to see we had a helper.

"Only rich people have maids," she said.

I explained, "We have a helper because we are poor. Dad and Mom both have to work to make ends meet."

She became as enthralled with Neelie's cooking as we were.

On a visit after our marriage, Diana asked, "Neelie, can you tell me the recipe for one of your cobblers?"

Neelie replied, "Honey, I ain't got no recipes. I just put in a little bitta this and a whole lotta that."

Truth is, she had all the recipes in her head. She just didn't know the measurements. I must add at this point - Diana eventually became an excellent cook. Maybe, partly, because of the time she spent in the kitchen observing Neelie "concoct" her dishes.

Since Neelie went home after lunch, and both my parents worked until 5:00, I was a "latchkey kid" from fifth-grade through high school. That's "a whole 'nother story," which I'll tell later.

Our three children, Noel, April, and Jana also met Neelie. When we came for a visit to Livingston, after Noel was born, Neelie would sit in her usual chair at mealtime and hold Noel in her plentiful lap. She alternately cooed, talked, and sang to him, as he gazed lovingly into her face. Later, when Noel could walk, April became the babe in arms to be soothed with Neelie's melodious chatter.

Before Jana was born, Neelie, in her late 60's, became ill and had to quit working for Mom and Dad. They had paid her well, and her 25 years of salary helped finance the education of several children and grandchildren. We hated to see her go and grieved at news of her death years later.

However, while Neelie was lying sick and near death, Jana and I visited in her home. We brought her a love gift to help celebrate her last Christmas season and prayed for her.

You know what? It's possible for people to love and respect one another while acknowledging their differences. We didn't pre-judge Neelie, and I don't believe she pre-judged us.

Television in the 1950s

In 1950, just under 20 percent of American homes contained a television. Our home was not yet one of them.

I was already in junior high when we finally got a television in 1955. Black and white, of course, it sat on a TV stand with "rabbit ears" antenna on top. Our remote control was named "Johnny," as in:

"Johnny, get up and change the channel."

"Johnny, go adjust the rabbit ears" (for better reception).

"Johnny, go turn up the volume."

Being the remote, I made several trips from couch to television.

Broadcasting began at 6:00 a.m. with the Indian-Head test pattern, waving American flag, and "The Star-Spangled Banner." Stations signed off around midnight in the reverse order - national anthem, flag, and test pattern. Then "snow" - a white/blank screen for the rest of the night. That Indian-Head test pattern, a relic of early television days, had graphics and a picture of an Indian chief in headdress. Broadcast engineers used the graphics to confirm quality of broadcast.

"Why sign off?" you ask.

The stations simply didn't have enough content to fill up 24 hours. Besides, few people would stay up to watch anyway.

Broadcasting usually started with the news and ended with the news. We trusted the reporting of Dave Garroway, Edward R. Morrow, Walter Cronkite, John Cameron Swayze, Chet Huntley, and David Brinkley. They gave us the facts without their opinions. Journalists were professionals back then, and didn't feel the need to "spin" their reports for personal, political, or financial gain.

Some of our <u>favorite programs</u> were:

Your Hit Parade – Seven of the top-rated pop songs performed with elaborate sets and costumes.
Among our favorite songs on the Hit Parade were:
> The Everly Brothers' "All I Have to Do Is Dream"
> Perry Como's "Catch A Falling Star"
> Tennessee Ernie Ford's "Sixteen Tons"
> Rosemary Clooney's "This Ole House"
> Elvis Presley's "Hound Dog"

Amos and Andy – They were almost as good on TV as on radio. George "Kingfish" Stevens' catchphrase, "holy mackerel," entered the American lexicon.

The Dinah Shore Show – A variety show with music and comedy. Dinah ended each show with a musical encouragement for us to "See…the…USA, in your Chevrolet. America is asking you to call."

Caesar's Hour – Comedy sketches and variety with Sid Caesar and others.

Dragnet – Like the radio version, embellished with visuals. Sergeant Friday often said, "All I want are the facts, ma'am."

You Bet Your Life – A comedy/quiz show highlighted by Groucho Marx's witty remarks and facial contortions as he interviewed contestants.

The Honeymooners – Jackie Gleason (Ralph Kramden) a bus driver, and his best friend Art Carney (Ed Norton), a sewer worker, starred in comedy sketches about two couples struggling to make ends meet, while living in a low-rent Brooklyn apartment. Ralph often clenched a fist at wife, Alice, and said, "One of these days, Alice…Bang! Zoom! You're going to the moon."

*The Life of Ri*ley – William Bendix coined the catchphrase, "What a revoltin' development this is." He had a penchant for turning mere trouble into near-disaster through his innocent bumbling.

I Love Lucy – Lucille Ball entertained us with her crazy schemes and humorous antics.

Other favorite TV comedians were:
Jimmy Durante - who closed his program with "Good night, Mrs. Calabash, wherever you are." Her identity remained a mystery until 1966, when Durante revealed that it was his pet-name for his first wife, who died in 1943.

Bud Abbott and Lou Costello of "Who's on first?" fame.

George Gobel, Red Skelton, Jack Benny, and, of course, Bob Hope.

Dad and I loved watching baseball and football. Mom liked the baseball OK, but didn't care for the "primitive head butting and body mangling," as she described football.

Some of the future Baseball Hall of Fame greats entertained us. I hoped that by observing and imitating their skills I would follow in their cleats someday. It never happened, but the memories still linger. We became acquainted with the mannerisms, quirks, and unique talents of these bigger-than-life heroes. I'll name a few:

Ted Williams – Outfielder – Boston Red Sox
Bob Feller – Pitcher – Cleveland Indians
Jackie Robinson – 2nd baseman – Brooklyn Dodgers
Roy Campanella – Catcher – Brooklyn Dodgers
Stan Musial – Outfielder – St. Louis Cardinals
Roberto Clemente – Outfielder – Pittsburg Pirates
Yogi Berra – Catcher – New York Yankees
Mickey Mantle – Outfielder – New York Yankees
Ernie Banks – Shortstop – Chicago Cubs
Willie Mays – Outfielder – NY/San Francisco Giants
Hank Aaron – Outfielder – Milwaukee Braves

Dad and I also enjoyed the head-butting and body mangling of the National Football League on Sunday afternoons. I don't remember having a favorite team or player, but I do remember the bets Dad and I placed on the games.

Since only one NFL game was televised on Sundays, we took turns picking the winner and placing our bet. The payoff was extracted the following Sunday morning before Sunday School. The one who chose the loser of last week's game had to shine both pairs of shoes. The loser/shoe-shiner then had first choice for that day's game.

Dad must have done a lot of research. Maybe he knew how to read the bookies' odds, because, as I remember it, I did a lot of shoe-shining during those years.

Some of our favorite "warriors," later inducted into the Football Hall of Fame, included:

Sammy Baugh – Quarterback, defensive back, punter – Washington Redskins
Bobby Layne – Quarterback – Detroit Lions
Jim Brown – Running Back – Cleveland Browns
Lou Groza – Tackle / Kicker – Cleveland Browns
Elroy "Crazy Legs" Hirsch – Half back / flanker – Los Angeles Rams
Bart Starr – Quarterback – Green Bay Packers
Johnny Unitas – Quarterback – Baltimore Colts

In those days, you had to pay close attention to the baseball and football games - no pause button or instant replay. You snooze, you lose. Also, no long TV commercials.

It felt like being right there at the actual game - minus the inclement weather, fans blocking your view, and uncomfortable seats.

However, your view was like from the upper seats in the stadium. You couldn't zoom in to look up the pitcher's nostrils, watch the batter dribble tobacco juice down his chin, or examine the mangled football player bleed and grimace on the turf. Yep, viewing sports on old-time TV had its perks.

Viewing television in general - comedies, dramas, news, sports - became part of our daily routine. Thankfully, a "content rating system" was not needed. We never even imagined that someone would want to produce or even view programing with sexual content, profanity, and graphic violence. How things have changed!

Today, I'm glad to see that some of the old-time favorites are returning - in black and white, with good family values. They're still entertaining.

Latchkey Kid

As I explained earlier, Mom and Dad worked until 5:00 pm Monday thru Friday, and our helper, Neelie, went home after lunch. I came home after school to an empty, unlocked house. The latchkey is missing in this story. No need to lock up, probably because we didn't have much worth stealing.

We moved to our house on Calhoun in the summer of 1952, before my fifth-grade year. During the next eight years of school, I provided my own transportation to and from school, except in bad weather, when Mom or Dad taxied me to elementary school.

Our elementary school, the Alamo, was about a mile away from my house - as the bicycle flies. On the morning trip, my Schwinn bike and I struggled gallantly up a steep, block-long hill, followed by two blocks of level, black-top road.

Next were several blocks of paved and dirt roads winding through neighborhoods, and finally, a two block straight-away to the finish line. Coming home was a lot more fun, because the final stretch to the finish line was downhill. Like a horse headed to the barn, I couldn't wait to get home.

My trips to and from junior high and high school were easier, since both buildings were on one lot, only one block from our house. I walked. Like the dependable postman, "neither snow, nor rain, nor heat, nor gloom of night" stayed me from my appointed classes. No Mom and Dad taxi service.

My "home alone" afternoons were chock-full of activities. First, I finished my homework. Yes, you read that correctly. Believe it or not, I became a serious student in junior high and high school.

Sometimes friends and even smaller neighborhood kids came to join in some backyard activities. We enjoyed games of cops and robbers, ante over, football, baseball, basketball - you name it.

As a high school baseball player, I became the personal coach for Clippy, our next-door neighbor. He was six years younger than me, and aspired to be an infielder. Many afternoons I worked with him on fielding grounders. I found out years later he became the starting second baseman in high school. That was fulfilling.

You younger readers may be asking, "That's all you did? What about watching television and talking on the phone with your friends?"

Nope. No TV or telephone in the afternoons - not a rule, but a choice. I'm so thankful we were deprived in the 40s and 50s of video games, cell phones, and social media. Having to make our own fun, we learned creativity and social-interaction. Yep, I have fond memories of being a latch-key kid.

FINDING A CAREER

You can't stay in high school forever, which would have been my first choice. I had friends, baseball, church, and the promise of a new summer job at the Texas Highway Department. Life was good.

But they don't let you stay. After graduation you must move on and find a career. That's what I lacked - an idea for a career. Not because I didn't want one. I just couldn't decide what mine would be.

In junior high, a teacher asked us that awkward question, "What do you want to be when you grow up?"

"I don't plan to grow up," was my first thought, but that probably wouldn't be a wise answer.

Spoken answers included:
"I don't know."
"Rich."
"Not in jail."
"Huh?"

A few kids gave good answers. There were future doctors, lawyers, teachers, firemen, and ditch diggers.

When it came my turn, I hesitated to express my dream to be a Major League baseball player. The raucous laughter would have been too humiliating. So, I proudly announced, "I will probably go into the oil business."

It sounded impressive - like maybe I would have some oil wells and become a millionaire. My close friends knew what I meant. I would drive a gasoline truck, delivering gas and motor oil to stations in the county. That's what Dad did, and I assumed I would follow in his steps.

Years later, as high school graduation approached, I reviewed my resume'. It was somewhat short on useful experiences and marketable skills.

In the third grade, my friend Mack and I had a short-lived career in manufacturing glue. We had discovered, in the woods near his house, some vines which oozed sticky slime. We fantasized collecting the goo in bottles and selling it for glue. Never happened.

In the fourth grade, Jimmy Windham, William Close, and I formed a used motor parts business. Taking the initials of our names (W, C, J), we named it "We Collect Junk."

Back then, gas stations also had a repair garage and a mechanic, and we discovered that behind many of those garages, one could find a treasure cove of discarded auto parts. We started collecting them, with the plan to repair and resell. Never happened.

In the fifth grade, I became a twice-a-week lawn mower, using our heavy, hard-to-push, gas powered mower. Our house sat on one lot with a front, side, and back yard full of grass. A second lot in the back was all grass. Our neighbors' setup was identical.

I mowed our yard and back lot once a week for free, and the neighbors' every Saturday for $1.00. Mowing, raking, and bagging one yard took about three hours. I still mow my own yard, because I just can't find anyone to do it for $1.00.

In the sixth grade, I began learning "the oil business," going to Gerlach Bros. warehouse with my dad on Saturdays, and often during the summers. I learned to drive an 18-wheeler, going only forward and backward a few feet in the parking lot. I also learned how to man the office alone and do the books. I enjoyed being with my dad, but I was not destined to be an "oil man."

In the seventh grade, I learned to play poker. My ability to cut the cards using only one hand was impressive, but I lost too many match sticks in the betting. Gambling never became a temptation, or a career option.

In the eighth grade, my friends and I went to dance parties with music provided by 45-RPM records played on a Victrola (some of you may need to Google that one). Four of us got the idea to form a Rock and Roll Band to perform at those dances. Fame and riches awaited us.

Problem was, none of us could play an instrument, so we improvised. We planned to borrow a set of drums, a guitar, a saxophone, and a bass fiddle and pretend to play them while lip-syncing the words. The actual music would blast from a Victrola hidden behind a curtain.

At practices, our gyrating with the make-believe instruments and pantomiming the lyrics was pretty cool, but the real instruments were not available for borrowing. We never approached our moms with our plan to have them design and create groovy R&R outfits. Our music careers ended on a sour note.

As a high school freshman, I joined a group of dancers that prepared for competition on a Houston TV talent show similar to American Bandstand. We practiced the Jitterbug for weeks as boy and girl partners.

My original partner was the best female dancer in the crowd, but I soon proved to be a poor match for her. She switched to a better partner, and I was paired with a girl of my equal agility. Sounds humiliating, I know, but at least we got to perform on live TV, competing with dancers from other schools. I never got a call-back for a repeat performance, so assumed my future career would not involve dancing.

After my freshman year, I painted our wood-frame house all by myself. It took most of the summer. Dad paid me a few dollars, and I developed some useful skills in painting, but that job convinced me I was not called to be a house painter.

So, with that short resume' in mind, I wondered what my "life calling" would be. What had my 12 years of schooling prepared me for?

From as long as I can remember, Mom and Dad encouraged me to save money for college. I assumed that meant I <u>was</u> going to college. They provided me a large, blue, book-like box with a slot in the top for inserting and saving money.

Through the years, I filled it several times with coins and bills and deposited them in a bank account they set up in my name. They also did some wise investing that provided more funds for college. So, the college question was never "whether to go?" rather "where to go?" and "what to major in?"

As I shared in "Darkness to Dawning," my sophomore year in high school set me on the path of searching for God's calling in my life. I fervently prayed every night before going to sleep, "Lord, what is Your will for my life - my calling?" Surely, God would shine a bit of light ahead on that path, so I could know and follow it. But He didn't, and I wondered why.

Other friends seemed certain of their college and career. One classmate even knew he was called to preach while still a junior, and was actively pursuing that career.

"Lord, why not me?" became my prayer. "Don't you want me to be a preacher or a missionary?" Silence.

Crunch time approached toward the end of my senior year, so I sought advice from several teachers and the guidance counselor.

"What do you think I should major in?" I asked them.

"You're capable of doing anything you want to," they replied. They must not have known me all that well.

I reluctantly asked some of my friends. They laughed. They did know me well. If there had been a yearbook category "Least Likely to Have Two Serious Thoughts in a Row," I would have topped the list every year.

Grades were not a problem. Faithful teachers had diligently prodded me to strive for A's. My friend, Martha, helped rescue me from a C in Spanish, and I ended high school with the highest GPA among the boys. Remember now, our class had only 52 graduates, and boys were expected to excel in sports, not grades.

So, what to do? I made a list of my skills and interests - both of them - math and outdoors. OK, it was a short list, but somehow it whispered, "Try Civil Engineering."

That's how I wound up a Longhorn at the University of Texas, enrolled in the Civil Engineering department, that Fall semester, 1960. I had found a career - or so I thought.

WHERE DO YOU STOP?

Where do you stop? What's enough when you're telling your life story of growing up in Poke County? A myriad of recollections crowd around the threshold of my memory demanding to be recognized and recorded, but I've got to shut that door. They'll just have to wait for another book to be written.

There, I've shut the door and locked it. But wait, I still hear knocking and screaming. Some of those memories won't go away. Persistent, pesky rascals! Scenes flash before me like a power point presentation. I started to say, "like a view-master or a slide show," but only old folks would understand those. OK, I'll crack the door open and allow a few of the more insistent ones in.

There I stand as a fifth-grader with phone receiver in hand. The phone is black and attached to the black receiver by a long black cord. It's our very first phone. There is no rotary dial or buttons to push. First, I pick up the receiver and listen to see if anyone is already talking on the "party line."

Oh, good - silence. I wait. The operator at the switchboard says, "Number please," and I give her the number I'm calling. Our number was 641-G. Some of my friends' numbers were 369 and 352-R.

Those phones were a lot more practical than the cell phones of today. We didn't carry them around with us to Text or Instagram our friends. We simply got together and talked, played, and interacted with the actual persons.

Our phones had no apps or games to draw us inside ourselves, away from the real world. We left our phones on the phone table at home and went outside to experience God's creation - our beautiful part of the land and the people He had put there.

Oh yes, there comes another memory sneaking through the crack in the door. I'm seven years old, riding my bike alone, full-speed, down a busy road near Aunt Tom's house. It's a Saturday, and I'm spending the day with her.

I decide to practice my "Look Mom, no hands" trick, when my front tire finds a crevice in the road. Bike and boy fly in different directions. I remember that part, but the next few minutes are a complete blank. I wake up lying on a bed in Auntie's house, where she and a burly truck driver are hovering over my limp body. They give me the full details.

Mr. Truck Driver, following behind me on the road, witnessed the horrifying accident. He stopped, picked me up, and knocked on the door of the nearest house. Auntie opened her door.

The man said, "Scuze me, mam. This little boy done had hisself a bike wreck. He tried to ride his bike with no hands and spilt hissef on the road."

"That's my nephew. Seems he's had another one of his accidents. Bring him on in."

They laid me on the bed and waited for me to regain consciousness. I did.

Afterwards, both Auntie and I thanked the truck driver for his kindness. I hoped he would stick around for a snack and maybe listen to the radio with me - anything other than leave me alone with Auntie, who was already rehearsing in her head the stern lecture she would lay on me.

Well, Mr. Truck Driver needed to resume his delivery, so I reluctantly told him "good-bye." Next came the scolding. Being a good Baptist, Auntie lacked the spicy vocabulary to punctuate her delivery, but it seared a sizable wrinkle in my brain. I never again tried "Look Mom, no hands."

"You forgot to include me," yell my memories of antics with Jimmy Defee.

His family moved to Livingston our junior year, and Jimmy and I became instant best friends. We shared a commitment to Christ and Central Baptist Church, a love of practical jokes, a passion for sports, and a weird sense of humor.

Once, Jimmy and I filled a friend's front yard with trash and a sign that read "Junk Yard." When his parents correctly identified the culprits, Jimmy and I cleaned it up ourselves. Joke backfired.

One dark Halloween night, we stood on opposite sides of a neighborhood street waiting for cars to come by. As one approached, we would extend our arms and jerk backwards as if drawing a rope taut across the road. Oh, the hilarity, as we watched cars come to a screeching halt, while we escaped into the shadows. One driver even got out of his car and tried to find the rope we dropped and left behind.

As college roommates for two years, Jimmy and I did even more outlandish things, which we will deny if ever found out.

There, that's all, I promise. Maybe another time I'll tell about:
* My snuff-dipping grandmother who lived with us during my sixth-grade year.
* My trips on the train with fellow elementary school kids to Houston to see the Shrine Circus and watch Roy Rogers and Gene Autry perform in the Fat Stock Show.
* My first date with my first girlfriend, my second girlfriend, and my third girlfriend - not all at the same time - I'm not that conniving.
* My friends and I hunting armadillos with baseball bats.
* My late-night yell, "Get my shotgun, Mom. Somebody's sneaking up on the front porch."
* Shooting Alfred with my BB gun.
* Rip - the world's dumbest dog.
* The day Jaime walked on water.

LEAVING POKE COUNTY

I've recorded for you the saga of my growing up years in Poke County. I wouldn't trade those years for anything. However, I needed to leave them behind and find new adventures outside my "comfort zone" of East Texas. On Monday, August 29, 1960, my folks drove me to Austin to enroll in the University of Texas and begin the next era of my life.

I'm so thankful to the Lord for my 40s and 50s upbringing in Poke County. I'm grateful also for my parents and family, and my friends and mentors who had part in that upbringing.

Although I returned to Livingston for three summers to work for the Texas Highway Department, I never really lived there again. The country-bumpkin from Poke County had moved on. But the flavor of the culture, the Biblical ethics of the society, the appreciation of the simple things of life, the memory of family and friends, and the southern drawl would stay with that country-bumpkin until he reached his 80's, maybe even longer.

WHAT'S NEXT?

Some sequels with these possible titles:
More Lore   College Lore   Foreign Lore
Watch for them.

A FINAL NOTE

Did you catch the anagram in the INTRODUCTION? That guy thanks you for reading his book.

Made in the USA
Coppell, TX
20 November 2021